...roof table-tops made from coal. More jobs in the making!

s. **Power to turn** postwar wheels. More jobs from coal.

—from Coal?

...ving sulfa drugs, ...edicines, chemi- ...beyond imagin- ...esearch in coal.

After the war, there will be lots of opportunities. So, if you are on a war job, stay on it until Uncle Sam says it's finished. Victory must come first.

...l sheer, wrinkle- ...m coal. Sturdy ...himmering, fire- ...rom coal. There ...locomotives—in- ...nned steam-tur- ...ate on coal and ...smoothness and

...the demand for ...ods makes jobs.

...after Victory!

A Report on the Prospects for Postwar Employment In The Industries Served by

Chesapeake & Ohio Lines

Cleveland

CHESAPEAKE AND OHIO RAILW... NICKEL PLATE ROAD PERE MARQUETTE RAILW...

It's still coal that puts flavor in the roast

Like millions of other farm women, Mrs. Curtis now enjoys the convenience of a gas or electric range, along with refrigeration, a food freezer, running water, a power washer and all the other modern, labor-saving appliances.

But it's still coal that puts the flavor in the roast — bituminous coal, used efficiently in a distant power plant. America's public utilities are burning more than twice as much coal today as they

did twenty years ago. Except in a few areas where other fuels are abnormally low in price, coal is the cheapest source of energy — cheaper even than water power. The TVA is now supplementing its great hydroelectric installations with coal-burning steam plants.

Another reason large fuel buyers favor coal is the assurance of continued supply. Even at our ever-mounting rate of consumption, known reserves are ample

for a future measured in thousands of years. These reserves are well distributed over the United States and great coal hauling railroads like the Chesapeake and Ohio are equipped to handle enormous quantities of coal promptly and efficiently.

Chesapeake and Ohio Railway

COAL...FUEL OF THE FUTURE

Bring your fuel problems to C & O

As the world's largest carrier of bituminous coal, the C&O is intimately familiar with every phase of coal use. We have a large staff of experts who will gladly help you to locate the coal best suited to your needs, to help you use it most efficiently; to help get it to you promptly.

Write to: Coal Traffic Department Chesapeake and Ohio Railway 2165 Terminal Tower Cleveland 1, Ohio

Chesapeake & Ohio in the Coal Fields
of West Virginia and Kentucky
Mines - Towns - Trains

by Thomas W. Dixon, Jr.

The Chesapeake & Ohio Historical Society, Inc.
PO Box 79
Clifton Forge, VA 24422
1-800-453-COHS
www.cohs.org

Front Cover:

This fine rendering of a typical modern coal mine along the C&O, populated by a GP9 diesel switching hopper cars, is patterned after Island Creek Coal Company's big, modern tipple and preparation plant at Price, Kentucky, and was used on several C&O publications, including the 1961 Chessie Calendar.

Page *iii* Illustration:

A 1946 view looking down on Jenkins, Kentucky. (C&O Ry Photo, C&OHS Coll., CSPR-770)

Digital Image Production: Debbie Paxton
Copy Editor: John Smith
Book Layout and Design: Mac Beard

The Chesapeake & Ohio Historical Society, Inc. is a non-profit organization dedicated to the collection, preservation and dissemination of information about, and preservation and interpretation of the history of the Chesapeake & Ohio Railway, its predecessors and successors. The Society operates a full-service archives staffed professionally, sells a wide variety of models, books, pamphlets, full length books such as this, and a monthly magazine dealing with all aspects of C&O history.

The Society may be contacted by writing:

**The Chesapeake & Ohio Historical Society
P.O. Box 79,
Clifton Forge, VA 24422**

or calling toll free 1-800-453-COHS (Monday-Saturday 9am-5pm), or by e-mail at: cohs@cfw.com. The Society maintains a history information Internet site at www.cohs.org, and a full service sales site at www.chessieshop.com.

© 2006
Chesapeake & Ohio Historical Society

International Standard Book Number 0-939487-81-0
Library of Congress Control Number 2006934118

TABLE of CONTENTS

Introduction

This is the second book on this subject by this author. It is intended to stand alone or to be used in conjunction with the first volume, published by The C&O Historical Society in 1995.

The first volume illustrated typical operations on the Chesapeake & Ohio Railway in the coal fields of West Virginia, Kentucky, and Ohio, by showing yards and terminals, trains, and tipples, with particular emphasis on railway operations.

Some similar material is contained in this volume, all of which is different from the first volume. In this book there are more photos and data on the actual mines and tipples, and on the coal camps, or company towns, that were also an important element in how the whole structure of coal mining and transportation was set up.

The era treated is from the end of World War II until the mid-1950s. In this period coal operations on C&O reached a high point as America's postwar boom demanded ever larger quantities of the high quality metallurgical coal that was one of C&O's most lucrative products. Coal traffic for electric power plants continued and expanded over this time, as did the amount of coal being exported from C&O's huge Newport News, Virginia piers.

Also, a great amount of coal was being consumed at the beginning of this era for home and business heating. The conversion to oil, electricity, and natural gas began taking over from coal in these uses quite swiftly during this decade, and within a few years, this business was essentially gone. Another use for coal that disappeared during the period was as fuel for railroads, as most major railroads gave up on steam power and phased it out in favor of diesel-electric locomotives. By 1956 almost all steam was gone from Class I railroads. Only Norfolk & Western held out a little longer, and it was officially completely dieselized by late 1960. C&O ran its last steam locomotive in the fall of 1956.

This was the era when C&O's wonderfully effective public relations machine touted the line as "The Coal Bin Of America," and as the "World's largest originator of bituminous coal." It was both. In the pre-war year of 1939 C&O hauled 52,517,776 tons of coal, and in 1946, the first postwar year, this figure had risen to 72,530,152 tons. By 1956 the total was 84,452,510 tons.

The pattern of production and transportation was this: coal originated in southern West Virginia on C&O branches located in the New River, Winding Gulf, Coal River, and Logan coal fields, and in eastern Kentucky on the Big Sandy field. The loaded coal cars were assembled at several marshalling yards (see map on page 2 & 3) located within the coal fields and from there were dispatched to C&O's major yards, where it was classified and sent to destination.

C&O built and maintained a huge fleet of coal carrying cars, mostly of the 50- or 70-ton capacity hopper car. A few 100-ton-capacity cars were in service. Low sided gondolas also were used frequently, although this type of car was largely phased out for hauling coal by 1960.

C&O's major yard for classifying westbound coal was at Russell, Kentucky, where it built a sprawling facility beside the Ohio River, which became the largest railroad yard owned by a single line in the world. Eastbound coal made its way to Clifton Forge, Virginia, where it was classified and sent mainly to the ocean terminal at Newport News. Because coal had to be supplied to buyers in a particular mix of size and grade, it would be held in the cars at Newport News's huge yard, and as ships docked, the various types of coal were brought out of the yard and dumped into the ship. This was an inherently inefficient operation requiring that cars sit idle for long periods of time awaiting the arrival of a ship needing that particular blend of coal. This required a large number of cars since the average turn-around time for a car from the mine to the port and back was about 30 days.

The pattern of coal shipment that we see in the 1945-1956 era was basically unchanged from what it had been since the turn of the 20th Century. With the various market forces at work that have been alluded to above, this pattern would break down in the 1960s and 1970s, and an entirely new paradigm would emerge in the 1980s going forward.

C&O was long recognized as one of the best run, most efficient, best maintained, and highest quality lines in the United Sates. At roughly 5,000 route mines in the era we are discussing, it was of medium size, but because of the great amounts of money that it had made over the years hauling the basic commodity of coal, it was financially very well positioned.

The book is organized first to show the C&O's equipment and facilities in the cold fields, including steam and diesel locomotives, hopper cars of various types, and the marshalling and classification yards and terminals used to transport the coal from mine to market.

The sections following illustrate the environment of the coal mines and railroad branch lines including the towns and coal camps that were typical of the era when the business was highly labor intensive and jobs were in the lower pay scale. The last section of the book shows typical coal mines and tipples in the West Virginia and Kentucky fields (by this time the Hocking Valley coal field of southeastern Ohio largely had played out and was of no great importance in C&O's overall coal haulage picture),

I hope that this book will provide an accurate sample of how coal was mined and transported in the exciting and turbulent era of the first post-WWII decade.

I want to add a special thanks to Al Kresse who supplied the chapter on C&O hopper cars of the era.

Thomas W. Dixon, Jr.
Lynchburg, Va., June, 2006

Background

The Chesapeake & Ohio Railway traces its beginnings to the Louisa Railroad, a short line charted in 1836 to carry farm produce. By 1850 it had renamed itself the Virginia Central and had expanded westward to Charlottesville and southeastward to Richmond. By 1857 it had pushed westward to the foot of the Alleghanies (spelled with an "a" in Virginia), where it stopped until the end of the War Between the States, during which time it was an important Confederate artery both strategically and tactically.

After the war C. P. Huntington, one of the Central Pacific's "Big Four" in building the Transcontinental Railroad, became interested in C&O as a possible eastern link to a true transcontinental line he contemplated. With Huntington's backing the line was pushed westward through the new state of West Virginia, reaching the Ohio River in 1873 at the new city of Huntington. It was linked with other Huntington-owned lines in Kentucky and Tennessee, and by 1886 was part of a true transcontinental operation under one man's control. But by 1888 Huntington lost control and Morgan interests, supported by the Vanderbilts, took control. Under the leadership of M. E. Ingalls and George Stevens, as presidents over the next 30 years, the line was upgraded, expanded, and most of the branch lines in West Virginia and Kentucky were built. These branches would tap the rich coal lands.

By the late 1890s coal had become the main source of C&O revenue, as it would always remain thereafter. The hauling of this heavy commodity mandated the development of ever more powerful locomotives, larger cars, and better roadway. During the era C&O became a modern, efficient railway, powered by the best of the steam locomotive builder's art, and provided with a first class road bed laid with heaviest rail and stone ballast, strong bridges, and large terminals.

During the Great Depression of the early 1930s, when fully half of America's railroads were in bankruptcy, C&O not only continued its high level of performance but used the occasion of available labor and resources to rebuild and upgrade its roadway once again, to an even higher standard. C&O was not as affected as many other lines because coal was so basic that it was required even when other things were not. Although its traffic declined, the coal business held up even during the worst years. As a result, the C&O was admirably suited to its important role in the great traffic boom of World War II. With its major eastern terminal on the Hampton Roads Port of Embarkation, it carried troops and supplies for the European Theatre of War throughout the next four years.

Following the war, C&O was guided by its visionary Board Chairman, Robert R. Young a Wall Street financier who gained control of C&O and its affiliated lines (Pere Marquette and Nickel Plate). He used C&O as a platform for his forward-thinking progressive ideas about how the railroad industry could maintain dominance in transportation in the face of competition from good highways, airlines, and river barges. He introduced the slogan "C&O for Progress" which was the hallmark of all that he and the management team he introduced did. C&O was one of the best known railroads in the decade we are discussing because of Young's iconoclastic approach, and his superb public relations team, headed by Howard Skidmore out of the line's Cleveland, Ohio headquarters.

Although Young left in 1954 his legacy lived on in the form of the people he had placed in key positions on C&O, and the railway persisted in its forward thinking, fueled by the power of coal money. By 1963 it acquired and eventually merged the ancient Baltimore & Ohio, and the Western Maryland, to form the Chessie System of the 1970s. In the 1980s Chessie System merged with Seaboard System (itself a combination of the Atlantic Coast Line, Seaboard Air-Line, Louisville & Nashville, and Clinchfield railroads). The new CSX Transportation eventually acquired parts of the old New York Central and Pennsylvania, and today is one of two major eastern railroad systems.

The period of examination (ca. 1945-1956) begins with C&O operating only steam locomotives, and ends just as the last steam is replaced by diesels.

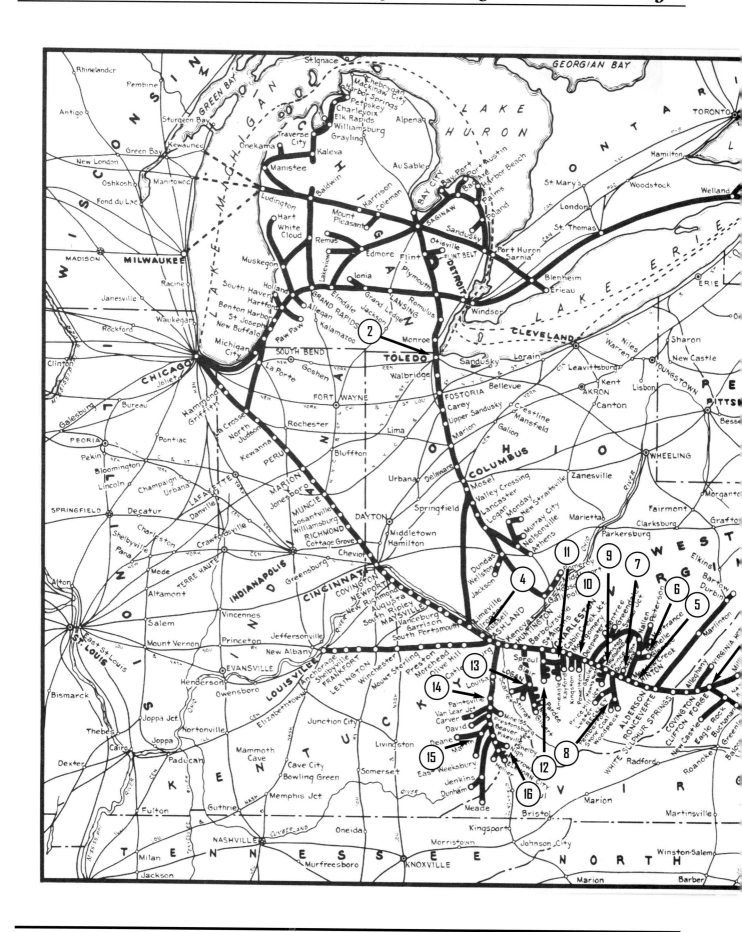

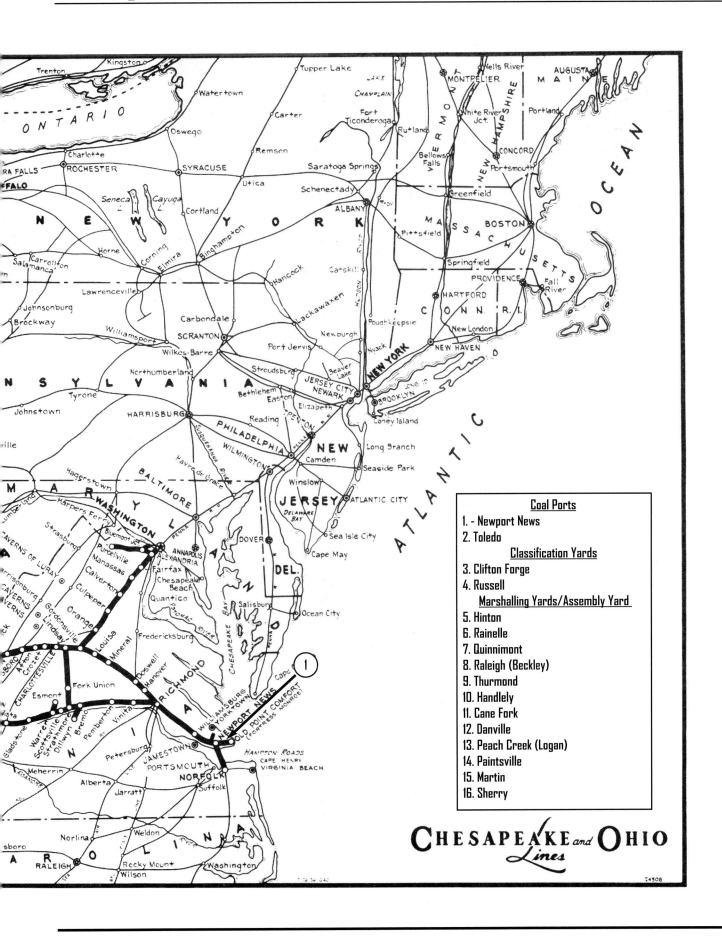

Coal Ports
1. - Newport News
2. Toledo

Classification Yards
3. Clifton Forge
4. Russell

Marshalling Yards/Assembly Yard
5. Hinton
6. Rainelle
7. Quinnimont
8. Raleigh (Beckley)
9. Thurmond
10. Handley
11. Cane Fork
12. Danville
13. Peach Creek (Logan)
14. Paintsville
15. Martin
16. Sherry

CHESAPEAKE *and* OHIO *Lines*

The C&O did not use its versatile K-4 2-8-4 "Kanawhas" (C&O named its 2-8-4 for the Kanawha River whereas most railroads, which called them Berkshires) for mine runs, but they were often used in pulling long coal trains from marshalling yards to main-line classifying points. Here No. 2723 is eastbound out of Russell, Ky., with empties for the coal fields. Note the box car behind tender and three more box cars spliced in the train. This often occurred as general freight was being sent to coal-field stations not served by regular freight trains. (Jeremy Taylor photo, C&OHS Coll.)

Chapter One

Coal Fields Motive Power

Steam

During the period before 1951, most mine runs from the marshalling yards were handled by 2-6-6-2 compound articulated Mallet type locomotives. With their short rigid wheel bases but great tractive power, these engines were ideally suited for the curvy branch lines, which sometimes had axle loading limitations of bridges as well. The Mallets could handle heavy loads during their shifter runs from mine-to-yard-to-mine, and if needed could be doubleheaded for additional power.

At the marshalling yard, switching was done by the available 2-6-6-2s, or by heavy switch engines. In all cases the switchers used were 0-8-0s except for the Peach Creek yard at Logan, W. Va., which was served by the C&O's giant 0-10-0s, the largest, heaviest, and most powerful switch engines ever built.

Once assembled at the marshalling yard the heavy coal train could be taken to the classification yard by H-4,5, & 6 class 2-6-6-2s, K-4 class 2-8-4s, or H-8 class 2-6-6-6s, depending on grades and other conditions. Leaving Hinton eastbound all coal trains would have an H-8 road locomotive and another H-8 pushing as far as the summit at Alleghany, Va. Westbound from Handley H-4, 5, & 6 Mallets were often used to take trains to Russell, however, K-4 2-8-4's were most common. Leaving Peach Creek yard 2-6-6-2s or 2-8-4s were the standard.

The usefulness of the 2-6-6-2s was illustrated

when C&O placed its very last steam locomotive order (delivered 1949) for a second H-6 class that became the last steam locomotives built for domestic use in America by a commercial builder (N&W had later locomotives that were home built). These locomotives were hardy changed in design and concept from those of 1920. They were just perfectly suited to the mine run work.

Trains leaving the classification yard at Clifton Forge headed down the gently descending grade of the James River and Rivanna Subdivisions, and a large train of 125 cars could be handled by an early 1920s era 2-8-2 Mikado, or occasionally a K-4 2-8-4. Leaving Richmond on the last leg of the trip over the Peninsula Subdivision to Newport News, K-4s and H-8s were used, and in the very last years of steam the huge T-1 2-10-4s and old H-7 simple 2-8-8-2s were used in this region.

Westbound from Russell, the big trains, aggregating sometimes 14,000 tons used either an H-8 or a T-1. The T-1s had been built in 1930 expressly for use in this service from Russell to Toledo. K-4 s were also used in this region.

Operationally, coal trains were run as extras from marshalling and classification yards whenever the traffic warranted. Train sizes were generally measured in numbers of standard 50-ton cars. Coal trains were most often run without any other cars being mixed in. However, in the coal branch region, the mine shifters would often take box cars and other local fright bound for the mine towns as part of their daily work. Photographic evidence also shows that box cars and flat cars could be

The C&O's magnificent H-8 2-6-6-6 Allegheny type was never seen on a coal branch, but it was constantly in use in the coal regions hauling heavy trains from mainline collecting yards to the classification points at Russell and Clifton Forge, and from there onward to Toledo or Newport News. Capable of the heaviest work, these great locomotives were at the top of the motive power scheme for C&O's coal traffic. (C&OHS Coll.)

seen in mainline coal trains on occasion.

Once a coal train had been made up and dispatched out onto the mainline it, of course, shared track with passenger trains, local freights, work trains, and fast through freight trains. On the coal branches the mine shifters were often the only trains operated. Almost every coal branch had a local passenger train that would complicate their shifter runs somewhat until most branch passenger service was discontinued in 1949.

Diesels

When C&O began buying diesels, it tried a number of builders, including American Locomotive Company (ALCO), Baldwin, and General Motors Electro-Motive Division (EMD) models. In the early dieselization period (1950-56), all of these models had a place in coal train operations. The new road switchers produced by the major builders were well suited to the mine shifter business. But even the F7 road units came down the branch lines to pick up trains at major marshalling yards. Ultimately the GP7 and GP9 EMD road switchers became the standard power, much as the 2-6-6-2 Mallets had been in the stream era.

For mainline coal trains eastbound from Hinton to Clifton Forge three to five GP9 units were used until the coming of the second generation diesels in the 1960s. From Clifton Forge to Richmond and Newport News, the GP7s and GP9s held sway again. Westbound from Russell, coal trains could have GP7s and GP9s, but F7s in ABA sets were very common, as most of C&O's F7 fleet was headquartered at Russell for maintenance and the locomotives were used on all the five lines radiating from that busy terminal.

K-4 No. 2723 is taking empties eastward through Charleston, W. Va. in the spring of 1956. Seen here pausing for water, the train probably will go on east to Handley where the cars will be distributed to branch lines. Note two rebuilt composite hoppers behind the tender. (Ray Tobey, COHS Coll.)

H-4 2-6-6-2 No. 1395 is seen here running light near St. Albans, W. Va., headed for the small engine terminal/yard at Elk Run Junction, on the Coal River branch, in April 1954. Once at Elk Run, it will assume duties as a coal mine shifter. (Gene Huddleston, C&OHS Coll. (CSPR-1689)

Right side view of H-4 2-6-6-2 No. 1462 as it rests at the Rainelle, W. Va. engine terminal on the NF&G June 1954. The Nicholas, Fayette & Greenbrier Railroad was jointly owned by C&O and New York Central, with C&O operating on certain branches and NYC on others. Rainelle was the terminal point and marshalling yard, and also supplied a large business of finished lumber from the huge Meadow River Lumber Company's mill. (C&OHS Collection)

The H-6 and H-4 classes were the dominant mine run power on C&O coal branches. Here H-6 No. 1494 rests from duties at Peach Creek, W. Va. yard May 14, 1955, in the last years of stream operations at this last bastion of steam on the C&O. (John Krause, C&OHS Coll.)

Another C&O 2-6-6-2 class that was used in the coal fields was the H-5, but there were only 20 of the locomotives, so they are almost lost in the overall fleet of H-4s and H-6s. Here No. 1528 is at the Shelby, Ky. yard between mine run tasks November 1, 1952. The H-5s were USRA standard locomotives. (Arthur B. Johnson photo)

H-6 No. 1485 at the Handley engine terminal in the early 1950s was photographed on this bright sunny day by C&O's public relations photographer during a tour of the coal fields to get photos for use in various coal-related publications C&O used to advertise its prime commodity. (C&O Ry Photo, C&OHS Coll. (CSPR-5159)

Also classed H-6, but very much more modern than most in the class, were Nos. 1300-1309, which were delivered in 1948 and 1949. They were the last commercially built steam locomotives delivered in the United States, and spent their very short lives in mine run service out of Peach Creek serving the Logan Coal Fields. No. 1307 is being turned at the Peach Creek roundhouse August 3, 1953 (August A. Thieme photo).

Although C&O had only 20 of the USRA-designed H-5 2-6-6-2s they were actively used in coal fields operations alongside the standard H-4 and H-6 classes in mine run service, as well as on mainline trains. Here No. 1538 is pushing an eastbound train of Logan coal eastward over the steep grade near Teays, W. Va. on the Kanawha Subdivision mainline. According to photographer Gene Huddleston, 1538 followed the train until it stalled, then coupled to caboose 90296 and shoved it to Teays, in February 1951. This is one of the C&O pusher operations not often illustrated. (Gene Huddleston, C&OHS Coll., COHS-1772)

In 1952, H-4s 1419 and 1331 work the small yard at Meadow Creek, W. Va. where coal from the NF&G line was brought to the mainline. (B. J. Kern, C&OHS Coll., (COHS-2766)

Of all the switch engines which served C&O, the 0-10-0s are by far the most impressive, and they were purchased solely to handle the very heavy work occasioned by coal operations. Most of them stayed at Peach Creek Yard and it here that they were most often photographed. Right side view of No. 138 at Peach Creek in 1950. (C. A. Coulter, C&OHS Coll.)

0-10-0 No. 137 does its work at Peach Creek in August 1956 just one month before the end of all steam on the C&O. (Gene Huddleston, C&OHS Coll., (COHS-1086)

C&O Engineer Carl A. Coulter snapped this photo of an 0-10-0 working at Peach Creek from his locomotive in about 1950. (C. A. Coulter, C&OHS Coll.)

The mighty H-8 2-6-6-6 Allegheny type was, of course, never used on the coal branches, but it was among the most common locomotives to be seen in the coal region, pulling the heaviest of mainline coal trains. Here 1626 works hard near Cotton Hill, W. Va., on the New River Subdivision main line in 1947. (C&O Ry. Photo, C&OHS Coll. (CSPR-1025).

This nice slightly overhead view of H-8 1627 with a coal train along the New River near Thurmond, W. Va. in 1956, as it worked out its last months of service. (C&OHS Coll.)

H-8 No. 1624 is eastbound with coal passing the Thurmond Depot in September 1955. The huge tender dwarfs the following 50-ton hopper cars! (Gene Huddleston, C&OHS Coll. (COHS-1898)

The other side of No. 1307 is seen in this photo at Rainelle, W. Va., on the NF&G in September 1950. Although the class was used almost exclusively at Peach Creek, they did, apparently, get work at other locations as well. (Paul B. Dunn photo, C&OHS Coll. (COHS-2147)

0-8-0 switchers were used at some of the coal fields marshalling and assembly yards, as C-16 No. 179 is in this photo at Peach Creek yard on May 23, 1956, the last year of steam operations on the C&O. (C&OHS Collection)

C-16 0-8-0 No. 190 works the Handley, W. Va. yard in March 1956. Handley served as the division point between the mainline New River and Kanawha Subdivisions, and was also a collecting point for coal from various branch lines. Generally 0-8-0's were powerful enough to handle the long strings of coal cars they had to manage at the various yards.

Not satisfied with the great power of 0-8-0s, the burgeoning C&O thought it needed something even bigger to handle the heaviest coal switching work, and received the massive Class C-12 0-10-0s in 1919. They could handle whole trains of coal if needed, and initially worked at Clifton Forge, Russell, and Peach Creek. In later steam days most of them congregated at Peach Creek. Here No. 141 is seen at that location in the twilight year of 1955. The monstrous boiler atop the seemingly tiny 50-inch wheels made the locomotive look top-heavy, but regardless of it's ugliness, it had superb power. (John Krause, C&OHS Coll.)

Among C&O's first diesels were of the F7 Road Freight or "cab" type and were built for use on through trains not involved in switching, so they were never used on mine runs, but they were used for powering coal trains from marshalling yards to the main-line junctions and to the classifications yards. Here a matched ABA set of F7s takes a heavy coal train west along the Levisa Fork of the Big Sandy River on the Big Sandy Subdivision near Prestonsburg, Ky., about 1954. Once the train reached the main-line at Barboursville, W. Va. it would continue to the big classification yard at Russell. (C&O Ry Photo, C&OHS Coll. (CSPR-3367)

Some odd combinations of diesels were used to carry coal from the marshalling yards, including this 4-Unit EMD TR4 set seen here with a mine run at Dawkins, Ky. in June 1958. (Gene Huddleston photo, Coll. of H. H. Harwood, Jr.)

Although GP7s were not initially intended for coal field work, they often appeared in that service as the years went by. Here No. 5784 waits at the Peach Creek engine terminal in 1972 while in use on mine runs. (T. W. Dixon, Jr. photo)

ABOVE - As C&O began buying diesels, it patronized several builders. From ALCO it received that builder's RSD-7 model. Seen here in company with H-4 No. 1490 during the steam-diesel transition period in April 1956, No. 6805 prepares to take empty cars up the Coal River Branch. Initially the RSD-7s were used to replace 2-6-6-2s one-for-one. Most of them congregated, with ALCO RSD-12s, at Handley and Peach Creek. (Gene Huddleston photo, C&OHS Coll. (COHS-1299)

RIGHT - A set of 2 GP9s must be at the limits of its strength as it powers a loaded coal train away from Big Sandy coal fields in 1964. The versatile GP9s were used on mine shifters and just as easily on big coal trains like this one headed to the classification yard at Russell. (C&O Ry Photo, C&OHS Coll. (CSPR-5026)

End view of C&O 107182 being pushed up to the rotary car dumper at C&O Presque isle Coal pier No. 1 at Toledo, Ohio, in 1954. C&OHS collection.

Chapter Two

Coal Fields Rolling Stock

by Al Kresse

Builder's photograph of the standard 33 foot, 50-ton C&O offest-side, twin-hopper car number 58546 at American Car and Foundry Company, Huntington, West Virginia, in 1945. These were built right after the war. COHS 8249.

After the second world war the C&O was left with an aging fleet of 1920s 70-ton hopper cars and 50-ton offset twin hopper and high-side flat-bottom gondla cars that were ready for major repairs or rebuilding. Cars purchased during the war were built to wartime emergency materials standards to save on higher strength steel that resulted in composite steel-wood construction hopper cars.

The era after the war will see a tougher look at weight reduction by reducing plate thicknesses and increasing steel tensile strengths and corrosion resistance. They were also looking at cost savings via welding cars together. This would save both the mass of overlapping rivet joints and fabrication man-hours.

The C&O was still using flat-bottom gondola cars to carry coal during this era. These 40-foot, 50-ton cars had a volumetric capacity of 1,976-1,980 cubic feet. Over ten thousand of these cars were still in use at the end of this era. The last three series of these were built in 1948, 1953, and 1958. Their use declined rapidly in the mid-1960s.

Their flat bottoms allowed them to be used as a general purpose car. The standard hopper car was still the 50-ton,33-foot, offset-side twin-hopper car. It would be made with or without end-extensions. The C&O picked up building these essentially to the same specifi-

cations as when the war started.

The wartime emergency constructed 50-ton twinhopper cars were soon rebuilt with high tensile strength, low-alloy steel plates replacing the wood panels. This happened in the early-1950s. The real changes happened in the 70-ton cars. Experiments were made with roller bearing journaled trucks. One-thousand cars were ordered in 1949 with Timken roller bearings. The goal was to minimize startup friction in the cold wheel bearings. These journals were more expensive and the operations folks wanted to see if they actually saved them fuel and reduced the needed starting tractive power. Therefore, they didn't become the industry standard until the mid-1960s.

The railroad car manufacturers had learned a lot about mass production techniques during the war and the steel companies now had lots of capacity for making alloyed steel plate. After the war, the C&O built lighter weight 70-ton cars than it did before the war. Sometimes, they overshot their target and had to make wider flanges or use plate another 1/16th of an inch thicker to meet durability requirements. The late-1940s and early-1950s saw new 70-ton coal cars stuffed with straw to fill cracks where welds had failed. They would go back to riveting until they got the designs and processes de-bugged. Today, these practices developed back then are the norm.

Old style 50 ton coal cars and new technology on conventional 70-ton cars

1935 built 33-foot twin-hopper car freshly repainted in the 1948 "C&O for Progress" monogram livery after shopping at the Raceland Car Shops in 1950. Phil Shuster photograph.

1943 wartime composite wood and steel twin-hopper car as it was rebuilt in all steel at Raceland in 1952. These cars retained exterior braces and ribs. Bob's Photo collection.

C&O 51158 offset-side, arched ends twin-hopper car at Lundington, Michigan, in 1953. Rebuilt at Raceland in 1952. Howard Ameling photograph.

Pressed Steel Car Company builder's photograph of a "typical" 40-foot C&O high-side gonodola number 36300 built in 1948. C&O HS collection

New roller bearing car C&O 79028 at Richmond, Virginia, in 1949. August Thieme photograph.

Fully loaded brand new welded, offset-top, ribbed-side, extended notched arched ends 70-ton car number 91131 at Island Creek, West Virginia, in 1948. 5500 similar all-welded cars were built in 1948 and 1949. C&O HS collection negative CSPR 2907

C&O riveted ribbed-side, notched arched end-extensions car number 105255 at the Guyan Eagle Coal Mine No. 1 tipple ready for loading in June 1954. The details of the separate notched arched extentions sitting on the top sill is well illustrated C&O HS collection negative CSPR 10057-003

First Raceland Car Shops built 70-ton hopper cars.

Above is C&O 110809 fully loaded at Peach Creek, West Virginia, in June 1956. This car has the second generation "C&O for Progress" monogram with white Roman lettering livery. It is of a riveted contruction with the ribbed-side, notched arched end extensions design. It is part of C&O class HT, series 110000-115249. The cars built in 1957 had the modern Futura Demi-bold lettering style that carried on into the Chessie System era. Philip A. Shuster was the photographer.

What should be noticeable in these photos is that the 50-ton cars were loaded (heaped) with 60-tons of coal and the 70-ton cars were loaded with almost 80-tons of coal. As AAR data confirmed conservative extended bearing lives, cars built with these types of trucks and wheels, when rebuilt, or built, in the 1960s would be classified as 60 and 80-ton cars.

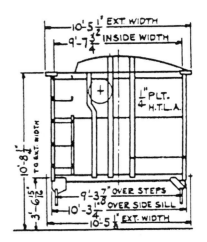

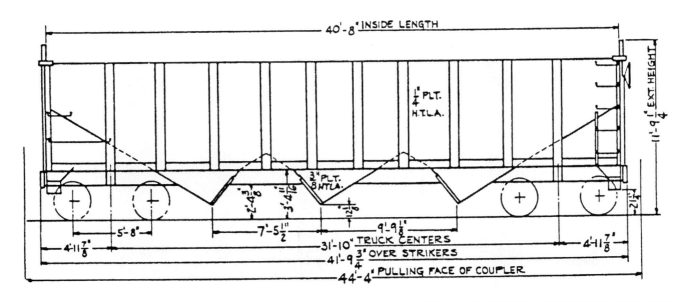

Coming down grade from Alleghany at Moss Run, Va., a set of five GP9s, headed up by 6261 takes a heavy coal train toward the large classification yard at Clifton Forge in September 1959. (C&O Ry Photo, C&OHS Coll., CSPR-4573).

Chapter Three

C&O Coal Operations

The eastern terminal for most C&O coal was Newport News. This aerial photo from the early 1950s shows thousands of cars loaded with coal waiting to be dumped into ships headed up the coast or overseas. (C&O Ry Photo, C&OHS Coll.)

Using the map which accompanies this Chapter and the map in chapter one, we see where C&O coal originated, where it was gathered, where it was classified, and where it terminated on C&O.

The C&O had two major coal destinations. Westbound coal terminated at Toledo, where it was dumped into Great Lakes shipping for transport to the industrial centers around the Lakes. Eastbound coal went to Newport News, Va. Situated on the great Hampton Roads harbor, opposite Norfolk, C&O reached this location in 1882, and since that time has been shipping coal up and down the coast, mainly to the New York and the New England states. Export of coal was a major market after World War II, much of it going to Japan and Germany during their rebuilding phase. Because of the good quality of C&O coal for steel making, the export market remained strong into the 1970s. Since then, the market has been up and down based on world energy and economic conditions.

There were two major classification yards. Westbound coal was classified for final delivery at Russell, Ky. in C&O's largest yard. From this point it was forwarded over the Northern Subdivision to Columbus, and thence over the Hocking Division to Toledo. Some coal was interchanged with the Nickel Plate at Fostoria. Although early shipments of C&O coal were mainly eastbound, once the Hocking Valley connection was developed the westbound flow soon exceeded the eastbound, and remained so in the era of our examination. Eastbound coal was classified at Clifton Forge, Va., where a hump yard was installed for this purpose in 1924. Here coal was arranged in blocks and given "Tide" numbers to identify it. The operators of the Newport News terminal would then use the blocks of "Tide" coal to assemble loads for ships and barges calling at that port.

Within the coal fields, C&O maintained smaller yards which are generally known as marshalling yards. These were located right in the coal fields, sometimes on the major branch lines, and were the hub from which empty cars were distributed to the mines of the region and loads picked up. This work was usually done with

This May 1948 photo shows the many varieties of coal hoppers in use on the C&O in several different paint schemes as they rest in the storage yard at Newport News. Gondolas were still used frequently for coal loads. (C&O Ry Photo, C&OHS Coll., CSPR-1439)

At the western end of the C&O coal routing were the docks at Toledo's Presque Isle facility on Lake Erie. Here coal of many different grades and varieties is awaiting transfer to Lakes shipping during the busy war year of 1944. (C&O Ry Photo, C&OHS Coll., CSPR-113)

what were termed "mine runs" or "mine shifters." A locomotive and crew would leave the marshalling yard usually in the morning with empties, and at each mine along the branch it would set off and spot the empties where the mine operation wanted them, and pull the already loaded cars from the mine tipple yard. By the end of the run the shifter would have a train of loads, which would then be deposited in the marshalling yard. It was at the marshalling yard that these cuts of cars would be made up into larger trains and dispatched to the classification yards. Major marshaling yards were: Rainelle, Quinnimont, Thurmond, Raleigh, Danville, Cane Fork, and Peach Creek in West Virginia, and Shelby, Martin, and Paintsville in Kentucky.

Two yards in West Virginia, Hinton and Handley, served mainly as mainline operational division points with major engine servicing facilities, however they also assembled coal trains. Huntington yard gener-

ally was not used for coal assembly.

If one were to observe coal trains operating over the C&O mainline in this era, east of Hinton loads would always move east and empties west. West of Russell, empties always moved west and empties east, and between these two areas loads and empties could be seen moving in both directions.

Facilities at the C&O's major terminals, including Newport News, Clifton Forge, Hinton, Huntington, Russell, Stevens (opposite Cincinnati), Parsons (Columbus), and Toledo (Walbridge yard) included roundhouses, coaling stations, water service facilities, shops for light repair, and large yards. Major repairs were effected at Huntington and Clifton Forge. The marshalling yards generally had a medium sized yard, engine house (usually the board-and-batten wood frame design), and scales for weighing cars.

An aerial view shows the extent of C&O's giant Presque Isle pier operation and its huge holding yard being worked by numerous steam switchers (see smoke plumes) in 1949. (C&O Ry Photo, C&OHS Coll., CSPR-797)

Chesapeake & Ohio in the Coal Fields of West Virginia and Kentucky

The classification yard for westbound C&O coal was at Russell, Ky. This photo shows the coal hump yard in the early 1950s. (C&O Ry Photo, C&OHS Coll., CSPR-2575)

Eastbound coal was classified at Clifton Forge, Va. Clifton Forge served three major purposes for C&O, first as the eastbound coal classification yard, second as the road's second major locomotive repair shop, and third as division point for three important subdivisions: the Mountain SD toward Charlottesville and Washington, the James River SD toward Lynchburg and Richmond (thence to Newport News) and the Alleghany SD to Hinton, W. Va. and the coal fields. Here cars abound in the coal classification hump yard in 1956. (C&O Ry Photo C&OHS Coll., CSPR-10393.169)

The main yard at Clifton Forge looking west is populated by coal in a wide variety of grades in March 1949. In the 1940s and '50s most coal loads looked like this, but from the 1960s onward coal loads are much more uniform, with most coal after that period being the small lump variety used for stokers and for industrial purposes. Note coal in gondola cars, as was a common practice in the period. The gondolas visible here have peaked ends and were specifically designed for coal loading (to be unloaded by rotary dumper). (C&O Ry Photo, C&OHS Coll., CSPR-2322)

This May 1948 photo shows an 0-8-0 working cuts of coal cars to make up trains at Handley yard. Note the wide variety of hopper car styles as well as gondolas in use. (C&O Ry Photo, C&OHS Coll., CSPR-1458)

ABOVE - C&O's mainline coal trains carried the product from the marshalling yards to the mainline terminals, thence to the classification yards, and then on to the ports. Here K-4 class 2-8-4 Kanawha type No. 2747 brings a coal train west near Huntington, W. Va. in about 1954, passing loaded cars on other tracks. (C&O Ry Photo, C&OHS Coll., CSPR-3182)

LEFT - Westbound coal is being taken from the marshalling yard at Shelby, Ky. toward Russell, as the H-4 2-6-6-2 Mallet powers it past BS Cabin as it enters the main line at Catlettsburg, Ky. in July 1945. (C&O Ry Photo, C&OHS Coll., CSPR-57.71)

An ABA set of matched F7s, led by 7046 takes empty hoppers eastward to the coal fields, on the mainline at Culloden, W. Va. in 1954. (C&O Ry Photo, C&OHS Coll., CSPR-10025.652)

In June 1957 an AB set of F7s, led by 7062 in the new simplified paint scheme, is captured here with eastbound empties at Blue Sulphur Springs, W. Va. on the Kanawha Subdivision. (C&O Ry Photo, C&OHS Coll., CSPR-2380)

K-4 2-8-4 Kanawha No. 2705 is seen bringing a loaded eastbound coal train into Handley, W. Va. in the later days of steam, about 1955. (C&O Ry Photo, C&OHS Coll., CSR-3399)

Loads are headed eastward toward Hinton, Clifton Forge, and the coast in this view. Five GP9s, headed by 5868 bring the long train around the sweeping curve past Cotton Hill, W. Va. station, on the New River Subdivision. (C&O Ry Photo, C&OHS Coll., CSPR-4543)

ABOVE - Not all C&O coal went off-line. Armco Steel's plant at Ashland, Ky. was a big consumer. This 1949 aerial photo shows the plant surrounded by piles of coal and ore. At one time Armco was the largest on-line C&O customer. (C&O Ry Photo, C&OHS Coll., CSPR-2447)

RIGHT - Another big consumer of coal that was situated right in the heart of the coal fields was the Appalachian Power Company's power generation plant at Cabin Creek, W. Va. This photo shows its huge pile of stored coal in the lower left corner. (C&OHS Collection)

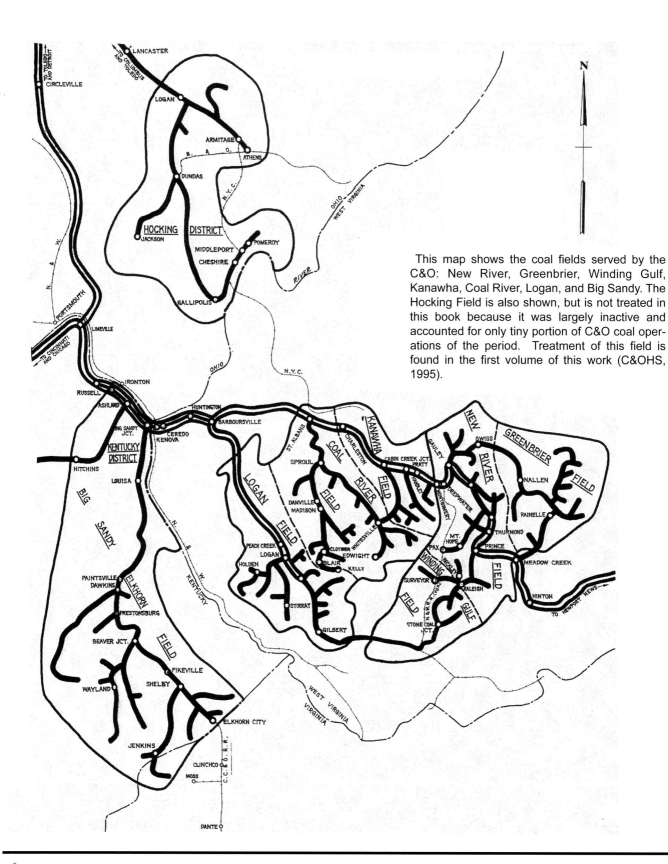

This map shows the coal fields served by the C&O: New River, Greenbrier, Winding Gulf, Kanawha, Coal River, Logan, and Big Sandy. The Hocking Field is also shown, but is not treated in this book because it was largely inactive and accounted for only tiny portion of C&O coal operations of the period. Treatment of this field is found in the first volume of this work (C&OHS, 1995).

Chapter Four

Coal Towns

A 1946 view looking down on Jenkins, Kentucky. (C&O Ry Photo, C&OHS Coll., CSPR-770)

The subject of coal company towns or "coal camps" has been fairly extensively treated in a number of excellent photo histories, concentrating on the towns of southern West Virginia along the C&O, N&W, and Virginian railways. At this writing (2006) several are available and in print. The purpose of this section in this book is not to treat this subject as exhaustively as the books mentioned, but to depict a few typical examples of how coal towns were situated, the types of structures

seen, and a general feeling for the environment around these towns.

Most coal towns were located very close to the actual mine sites, since miners could be expected to walk to work. A second reason is that most of the towns were owned and operated by the mining companies. This included providing the miners not only with a small house, but with the normal facilities of a small community such as a church, general store, movie theatre, and

This 1924 photo, taken from a panoramic view, shows the company housing at Sharples, W. Va., on the Coal River Subdivision. These houses are constructed with weather-board outer walls, tar-paper roofs, and each has a covered front porch (visible on back row) and a small covered back porch offset to one side. Neat two-door privies are also visible. (C&OHS Collection).

A part of the town of Raleigh, W. Va., a hub for C&O coal branch operations in the vicinity of Beckley, shows several rows of identical but very substantial two-story houses, as well as smaller square one-story residences. (COHS Collection)

A portion of another panoramic view, this of the C&O town of Kayford, W. Va., on the Cabin Creek Subdivision, shows houses of several different types, and the company store, which was always a large frame or brick building strategically placed in the town. Two C&O gondolas loaded with mine run coal await pickup. (C&OHS Collection)

perhaps another recreation hall of some type. The company store was where the miners could spend their pay for the necessities if life. Most mining companies paid their workers in scrip, their own private money that was good only in the company store. This tended, along with the company's ownership of everything else in their lives, to make the miners captive to their work situation.

Abuses in this system, of course, led to formation of the miners unions and labor troubles that were for so long endemic to the coal mining regions of the country.

Today, many of the old company towns survive, even though the mines are long closed and gone. One can easily observe by the way the houses are built and placed that they were once part of a "company town."

For modelers interested in the coal regions, recent years have seen the production and availability of a number of models in several scales of coal company houses, and even a nice church of the usual design. Every town was somewhat different in its look and in the type and style of houses there, but a they were generally

of board-and-batten or weatherboard construction, sometimes with undressed roughly cut lumber. Most were painted, usually gray or white. They afforded little trim, and usually had a covered front porch of some type. They were not large, and one can imagine that the living space within, especially for a family with children, was very cramped.

The C&O itself did not own housing used for miners, of course. That was left to the mining companies, but C&O did own housing in many locations for its employees, especially track laborers and foremen. The railroad-owned structures were usually of a sounder, more elaborate, and more permanent construction than the company houses.

The photos in this section are from the C&O Historical Society's collection and range in era from the 1920s through the late 1940s. A coal camp town of 1948 was not dissimilar from one of 1925. It was only in the 1950s and forward that the towns began to change to any extent.

This 1924 view of a portion of Jenkins, Kentucky, shows duplex housing, another type found in coal camps. (C&OHS Collection).

Another view at Jenkins shows both one- and two-story housing. (C&OHS Collection)

These houses at Vanetta, W. Va., on the Gauley Subdivision, are at the very crude lower end of the type, with unpainted board-and-batten siding. Taken in 1932. (C&OHS Collection)

The town of Elkridge on the Elkridge Subdivision off the Powellton branch in the New River field shows houses of different styles arranged along the dirt street separated by a chicken-wire fence. Note that the houses appear to be painted in gray with white trim. (C&OHS Collection)

Also on the Powellton Branch is the town of Kimberly, seen here with houses of several styles separated from the street/railroad by picket fences. The proximity of houses to mine operations and to the railroad is characteristic of the region. (C&OHS Collection)

This view of Crites, W. Va., on the Buffalo Subdivision in the Logan field, shows how the difficult topography of West Virginia constricted towns, mines, and railroads to a very narrow space. (C&OHS Collection)

McVey, W. Va. is the location of this arrangement of homes on stilts, again utilizing the available land to best advantage. (C&OHS Collection)

On the Horse Creek Subdivision in the Coal River District, the town of Breeze clusters along the C&O tracks. (C&OHS Collection)

These two details, taken from a panorama of Kingston, W. Va., located at the end of the Paint Creek branch, show very neatly constructed and well kept housing, the tipple, and a substantial church. One church building often accommodated many different denominations, each meeting at a different time. The substantial home on the hill is likely that of a mine official. (C&OHS Collection)

Laing, W. Va. is located on the Leewood Subdivision of the Cabin Creek branch, and is shown here in the 1920s, in this detail from a panoramic photo. The company store is visible at the left, while the town consists of one-story board-and-batten houses. The tipple of the Wyatt Coal Co. is in the distant murk to the right. (C&OHS Collection)

A miner and his children stand near their company house at Tams, W. Va. (Winding Gulf Subdivision) in 1945. (C&O Ry Photo, C&OHS Coll., CSPR-329)

The "Coal Miners Daughter" is pictured here by the C&O's photographer as he documented the coal fields territory at Tams in 1945. (C&O Ry Photo, C&OHS Collection, CSPR-328)

The miner's family is enjoying the air on their front porch in this 1945 view at Tams. (C&O Ry Photo, C&OHS Col., CSPR-331)

This 1954 photo shows Kayford's housing, overshadowed by the conveyor system for the Truax-Traer Coal Company's Raccoon Mine on the Cabin Creek Branch. Not much has changed since the earlier photo at Kayford shown previously in this chapter. (C&O Ry Photo, C&OHS Coll., CSPR-10057.Q01)

A 1944 view from the C&O's official photography file shows a nicely paved street with sidewalk at Wheelwright, Ky. (C&O Ry Photo, C&OH Coll., CSPR-178)

The Winding Gulf Coal Company's mine at MacAlpin, W. Va. dominates the town in this 1954 photo. Note that this is also a joint mine, with both Virginian and C&O hoppers under the tipple. (C&O Ry Photo, C&OHS Coll., CSPR-10057.F4)

This jointly served mine along the Stone Coal Subdivision has both Virginian and C&O hoppers under the tipple. Miner's houses are right next to the tipple in this scene from 1954. (C&O Ry Photo, C&OHS Coll., CSPR-10057.D04)

Pea sized coal is being dumped from the tipple at Vail into this C&O hopper as a mine employee observes and controls the conveyor. (C&O Ry Photo, C&OHS Coll., CSPR-3372).

Chapter Five

Mines & Tipples

This chapter depicts scenes that include mines and tipples on C&O lines. Most of these photos come from official C&O photos taken by the Public Relations Department for use in brochures, annual reports, and advertisements. Many of the C&O official photos of mines come from one photo trip that was conducted in June 1954, during which time the photographer on assignment took over 450 photos of mine tipples. Yet in all this photography, the tipple was the installation that was most often photographed. It was the focus of railroad activity at mines, with the coal being sorted, cleaned, separated, and then delivered by conveyor or chute into the waiting railroad cars. The photographer seldom ventured to the mine mouth, and we are left with few photos showing the operation of mines between the entry into the earth (either drift or shaft) and the arrival of the coal at the tipple. In this book and in the earlier work *C&O in the Coal Fields* (C&OHS, 1995), some photos showing the actual mining operation are presented.

In the tipple the raw coal came in from the mine mouth by car, conveyor, or bucket line and was then sort-ed, cleaned, and prepared for shipment. Several grades of coal were common in the era under consideration in this book.

Coal was generally graded into: slack (1/8th inch or smaller), pea, stove, egg, and run-of-the-mine. Coal cars of the era we are dealing with in this book (1945-1960) could be expected to be loaded with a variety of types when viewed in a train or in a yard. The pea or slack coal sizes were usually destined for businesses or homes that had large or small mechanical stokers for firing their boilers. Run-of-the-mine was the cheapest coal and also the hardest to handle, as it came in lumps of all sizes just the way it fell from the mine coal seam wall or face. Graded coal also was sorted meticulously by size using grates and by hand, and all impurities, such as slate or dirt, were removed.

As homes and small businesses moved away from steam and hot water heating and coal as a fuel, the appearance of coal in railroad cars changed as well, since most of what was mined began to go for power generation or other large steam production plants, or for steel

A maze of branches served mines out of the Raleigh marshalling yard, including some that were jointly served by the C&O and the Virginian. Here the Stotesbury No. 11 tipple is seen at Helen, W. Va. populated by Virginian hoppers. (C&O Ry Photo, C&OHS Coll., CSPR-10057.E08)

making use. This coal, much as it is seen in today's trains, looks about like the pea size of the earlier era.

In modeling a train or yard scene in the 1945-60 era that we are surveying, coal of all types should be depicted. A car of the big run-of-the-mine lumps with no uniformity could be hauled next to one with the uniform looking pea size, next to one with the larger lump stove grade, and so on.

Likewise, low side gondolas could be seen hauling coal on a regular basis, and C&O had a number of these cars with peaked or notched end extensions to allow heaping, as on the regular high-sided hopper cars. Hauling by gondolas was inherently inefficient because the volume of coal contained in a single car was not as great as it could be with the high-sided hopper, and at the point of destination it would have to be emptied by rotary dumper or removed by clamshell or manually by shovel. By the late 1950s very little coal was handled by gondola car. The 50- and the 70- ton, (and later 100-ton) hopper car became universal. Of course, in recent decades the hopper has been replaced in many cases by high sided "bathtub" gondolas that handle an even greater capacity than hoppers (but must be rotary dumped).

The C&O delivered empty cars to the mines as the mine shifter trains came out of the marshalling yard, and at the same time the loaded cars were picked up and taken back to the yard to be assembled into trains. Mine yards were built with a slight grade, so that mine personnel could move the cars by gravity from the empty yard under the tipple to be loaded, then out into the loaded side of the mine tipple yard. Generally only loads would be on one side of the tipple and only empties on the other. Few mines had a switcher of their own to move cars, as is common today. Most tipples had moveable conveyors that delivered the coal from the cleaning and separating area into the waiting cars, moving along the length of the car as it was filled. These were controlled by mine employees working in conjunction with others who may be seen in many photos watching the delivery of coal into the car. Sometimes photos show a mine employee collecting coal in a special container which he is holding under the conveyor. This was taken to the mine office for examination to ensure that the quality and size of the coal was correct.

Another element of coal operations was the supply of cars. A mine ordered the cars that it expected to use and the C&O would deliver them. This worked well unless there was a greater demand for cars than the supply available, so the C&O, like other railroads, had an elaborate car distribution bureaucracy that allocated cars to mines based on the history of their production.

The photos in this section are arranged by east-to-west along C&O branches in West Virginia and Kentucky, and are selected to give a representative sample of the variety of types and styles of tipples and operations that were there. More of these can be found in *C&O in the Coal Fields* (Published by C&OHS in 1995).

At the tipple, loaded mine cars are seen entering the dumping area and empties coming out. (C&O Ry Photo, C&OHS Coll., CSPR-335)

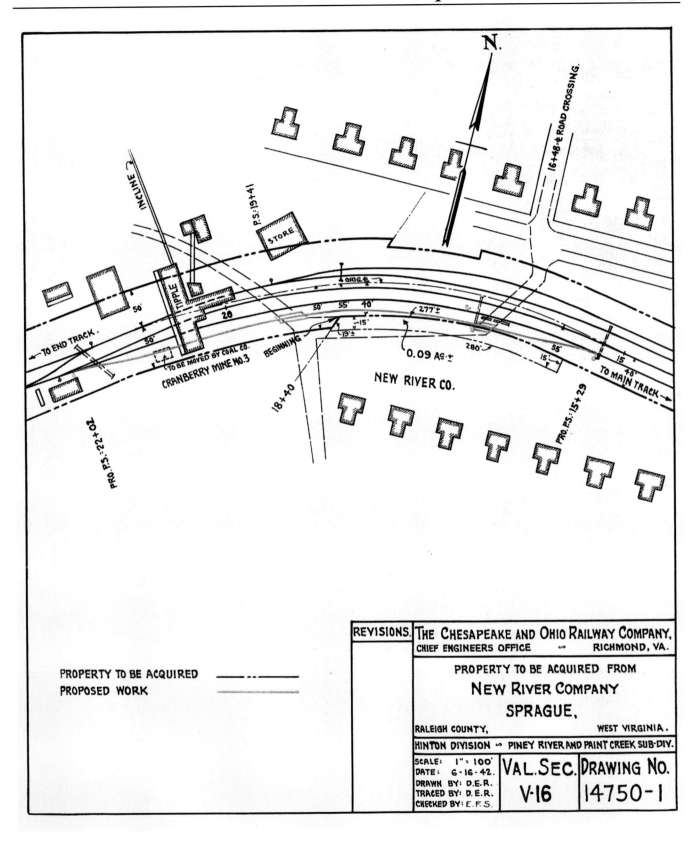

This 1942 map of the New River Company's Cranberry No. 3 Mine tipple and town at Sprague, W. Va. shows a typical mine tipple track plan. The map has been reduced by 10% for use in this book so if used for modeling the scale shown of 1" = 100 feet should be adjusted accordingly. (C&O Ry Drawing 14750-1)

This close-up of the Elkhorn No. 3 mine at Vail, Kentucky, on C&O's Dawkins Subdivision gives a good idea of how coal is delivered to the hopper cars under the tipple. The moveable conveyors are seen dropping coal into the waiting cars. (C&O Ry Photo, C&OHS Coll., CSPR-3369).

This scene at Guyan Eagle Mine No. 4 at Stowe, W. Va. in June 1954 shows well the different textures of coal loads. (C&O Ry Photo, C&OHS Coll. CSPR-10057.CC10)

The earliest coal mine operations on C&O were right along the main line through the New River Gorge, but by the early 20th Century a maze of branches had been built to reach deeper into the huge coal fields. By the era of this book most of the old mines along the mainline had played out and the branches supplied the coal. Here the Maryland-New River Coal Co., mine at Nutall, W. Va. illustrates the type of mine that was seen along the mainline in the New River, taken in June 1947. Note the long covered tram between the mine, high up the gorge, and the tipple. (C&O Ry Photo, C&OHS Coll., CSPR-1040)

C&O 2-6-6-2 No. 1465 has hoppers in front and back of it as it moves along the South Main Line (running from Sewell to MacDougal) to service the mine at Kaymoor. (C&O Ry Photo, C&OHS Coll., CSPR-1041)

This is one of few photos available showing a mine tipple operation on the Nicholas, Fayette & Greenbrier RR operation and shows Imperial Smokeless Coal Company's Quinwood #2 mine in June 1954. (C&O Ry Photo, C&OHS Coll., CSPR-10057.K06)

Quinwood #2 mine as seen from the side shows the shed in which the cars from the mine are dumped into the tipple at the top, and the main tipple sorting and cleaning structure at center. The tower-like building closest to the camera is where very fine slack coal was blown and stored. A very close examination shows a motor-truck under the tipple, possibly being loaded with coal for local use. (C&O Ry Photo, C&OHS Coll., CSPR-10057.K05)

This scene shows a 2-6-6-2 pushing empty cars upgrade on the NF&G at Top Siding in about 1950. Wooden cabooses were used on mine runs, and could appear anywhere in relation to the locomotive based on the switching being done. (Bernard Kern Photo, C&OHS Coll., COHS-2645).

Typical of coal fields marshalling yards, Rainelle, on the NF&G always hosted a gaggle of Mallets, and the facilities to service them. Its unusual engine house was a landmark. Water, sand, and cinder faculties are at right. A careful examination shows the tender of a NYC locomotive in the engine house. NF&G was a joint operation, though C&O had the bulk of the business. (Jay Williams Collection).

All coal operations were conducted in mountain-valley scenes such as this showing a train on the NF&G loops at Claypool, W. Va. in 1958. Three GP9s take loads down to the New River at Meadow Creek. The train will be on the line seen in the distance in a few minutes. (Gene Huddleston Photo, C&OHS Coll., COHS-3447).

The rugged New River is at left and the C&O double tracked main line at right as an eastbound coal train moves into the deepest portion of the gorge at Cotton Hill, in 1952. (C&O Ry. Photo, C&OHS Coll. (CSPR-3058)

Typical of New River Gorge scenery is this 1954 photo taken near Fayette, W. Va. where C&O hugs the bank of the river, as a coal train makes its way eastward. (C&O Ry Photo, C&OHS Coll., (CSPR-3397).

Typical of coal fields scenery an H-8 powers a westbound empty hopper train at Brooks, W. Va., just out of Hinton in about 1950, with a nice plume of exhaust on what must have been a cold winter day not so long ago yet of another world. (B. F. Cutler, C&OHS Coll.)

Typical of coal trains along the New River mainline in the mid-1950s-1960s era is this eastbound near Deepwater, in September 1959, with five GP9s (5969 in the lead). In the steam era this probably would have been powered by an H-8. (C&O Ry. Photo, C&OHS Coll. (CSPR-4555)

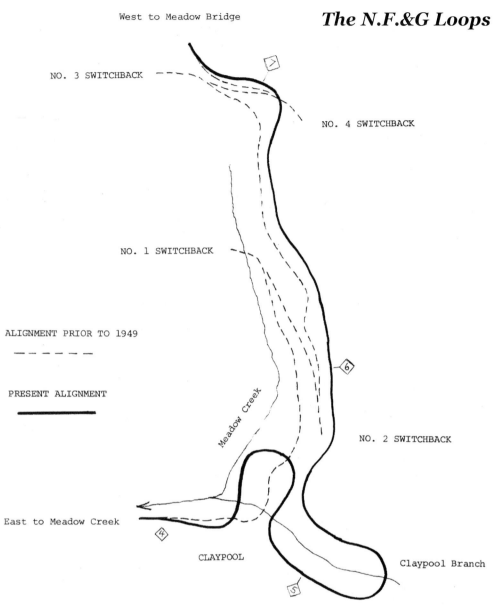

The N.F.&G Loops

West to Meadow Bridge

NO. 3 SWITCHBACK

NO. 4 SWITCHBACK

NO. 1 SWITCHBACK

ALIGNMENT PRIOR TO 1949

PRESENT ALIGNMENT

Meadow Creek

NO. 2 SWITCHBACK

East to Meadow Creek

CLAYPOOL

Claypool Branch

LEFT - An aerial view of the C&O's new loop tracks near Claypool, W. Va. on the NF&G shows how engineers eliminated switchbacks by re-routing the line in 1949. This certainly would fit a model railroad well. (H. H. Buster, C&OHS Coll. (COHS-9556)

ABOVE - The accompanying map shows the NF&G loops and the switchbacks that they replaced. (Map by Everett N. Young).

A more scenic spot for photography could hardly be imagined than the remote NF&G loops. Here two H-4 2-6-6-2s are taking an empty hopper train upgrade toward Rainelle. (B. J. Kern, C&OHS Coll. (COHS-2774)

A 2-6-6-2 in the distance works its empty hopper train up the loops in 1952. (B. J. Kern, C&OHS Coll., COHS-2772)

H-4 No. 1491 traverses the relative new loop tracks at Claypool in the summer of 1952. (B. J. Kern Photo, C&OHS Coll. (COHS-2773)

H-4 No. 1436 pushes backwards on a loaded coal train at Claypool in November 1952. (J. I. Kelly, C&OHS Coll. (COHS-20)

Another large Winding Gulf region tipple is this Lillybrook Coal Co, facility at Affinity, W. Va. with a C&O mine shifter run just visible in the foreground, in 1947. (C&O Ry Photo, C&OHS Coll., CSPR-1172)

Winding Gulf Coal Company's Crab Orchard operation is seen here in overhead perspective on the Raleigh & Southwestern branch in October 1945 as C&O 2-6-6-2 No. 1481 mine shifter pulls loads to take to Raleigh. The tipple has only three loading tracks, but seems to be producing a large amount of coal. The loads will go to Raleigh, will be made up in a train and taken to Quinnimont on the main line, and then picked up there and moved probably to Hinton and east. (C&O Ry Photo, C&OHS Coll., CSPR-357)

This close-up of the Crab Orchard mine shows mine-run coal being loaded. (C&O Ry Photo, C&OHS Coll., CSPR-356)

The other side of the Crab Orchard mine shows both Virginian and C&O empties, waiting to be drifted down under the tipple and loaded. (C&O Ry Photo, C&OHS Coll., CSPR-10057.G01)

A close-up shows a Virginian hopper being loaded at the Crab Orchard mine. Note that the conveyor has been lowered into the car. June 1954. (C&O Ry Photo, C&OHS Coll., CSPR-10057.G05)

LEFT - Typical C&O 50-ton offset side radial end and notched hopper cars are loaded with run of the mine coal at Crab Orchard mine in June 1954. (C&O Ry Photo, C&OHS Coll., CSPR-10057.G03)

LEFT - Lillybrook Coal Co. No. 3 mine is at Lillybrook, W. Va. on the Stone Coal district in June 1954. A Virginian hopper is under the tipple and three C&O offset side hoppers await loading. (C&O Ry Photo, C&OHS Coll., CSPR-10057.D01)

This overhead view of the C. H. Mead mine at Mead, W. Va. is on the Stone Coal branch, actually a part of the Virginian Railway but served jointly by Virginian and C&O. This June 1954 view shows both Virginian and C&O cars, the main tipple building and the conveyors bringing in coal from mine openings. Note the Virginian load and the C&O empties, indicating that the coal was headed in two different directions. (C&O Ry Photo, C&OHS Coll., CSPR-10057.D09)

Two coal trains meet on the Piney Creek branch, one taking loads down to Quinnimont yard and the other bringing empties up to Raleigh for loading, in October 1945, (C&O Ry Photo, C&OHS Coll., CSPR-308)

Four GP9s led by 6261 bring a loaded coal train off the Piney Creek branch toward the mainline, crossing the New River at Hawk's Nest, W. Va. in the early 1960s. The four Geeps replaced the single 2-6-6-2 Mallet taking trains to and from Raleigh. (C&O Ry Photo, C&OHS Coll., CSPR-11573.TB4)

Thurmond, the famous coal terminal in the heart of the New River Gorge was headquarters for coal coming down from a number of branches to the South. Here G-7 No. 975 and H-4 No. 1465 are parked on the track leading across the river to the coal branches in 1945. Used often as emblematic of Thurmond, this photo shows the depot (built 1905), which is now a major attraction of the National Park Service's New River Gorge National River. (C&O Ry Photo, C&OHS Coll., CSPR-301)

Thurmond was terminal for the Keeney's Creek branch, where small 2-8-0s were used because of the branch's light rail. Several were required because of the steep grades. Here G-9 No. 990 is returning with a mine run from Keeney's Creek in September 1953. The locomotive is backing into the Thurmond yard with the train. (Gene Huddleston photo, C&OHS Coll., COHS-1307)

Just west of Thurmond on the main line was the coal and coke operation at the junction of the narrow gauge Mann's Creek Railroad, which delivered coal to coke ovens at this point, and to the C&O. This photo shows coke being loaded through a small tipple, its conveyors supplied by coke drawn directly from the ovens onto the flat conveyor belt seen at right. This was one of the last beehive coke oven operations in the New River area. Photo taken in June 1954. (C&O Ry Photo, C&OHS Coll., CSPR-10057.H10)

The White Oak Subdivision was one of the lines served from Thurmond. The New River Company's Whipple mine has one of the ubiquitous C&O 50-ton offset side hopper cars loaded with huge lumps of coal up to the top of its radial end projections in this June 1954 photo. The tipple itself has a rather ramshackle look. (C&O Ry Photo, C&OHS Coll., CSPR-10057.B9)

On the White Oak line another New River Company mine was located at Oakwood and is pictured here in June 1954, a single heaped load of coal parked near the tipple. This tipple is similar to others of the New River Company, especially with the tall pulley mechanism. Note that the coal load is heaped but in distinct piles. Today's heaped loads are uniform because they are loaded as the car moves under a high-speed loader. In 1954 the car or conveyor would have to be moved several times to get the load positioned, sometimes giving a less uniform appearance. (C&O Ry Photo, C&OHS Coll., CSPR-10057.C01)

The Minden (also called the Rend) Subdivision was located on the south side of New River, just opposite Thurmond, on a very steep grade that originally required use of Shay geared locomotives in the early days of the 20th Century. This view of the New River & Pocahontas Consolidated Coal Company's Minden mine was taken as part of the big C&O photo-shoot of June 1954. It shows the coal in the mine cars in the foreground going into the conveyor, and the loads exiting the tipple into hoppers with a ball-in-square logo on it. This company was also known as "Berwind," and operated a fleet of about 1,000 private cars from this mine and others in the New River field. In the period of examination the Berwind cars were about the only private cars to be seen in C&O coal trains. (C&O Ry Photo, C&OHS Coll., CSPR-10057.CC03)

The New River Company's Garden Ground mine was located on C&O's Mill Creek Subdivision and again is photographed in June 1954. Some brand new C&O three-bay 70-ton welded hoppers have been loaded with slack. Note again that the slack is loaded under the tipple but other grades are loaded from extending conveyors. The C&O station sign is located next to a small board-and-batten structure which may have been a railroad structure. (C&O Ry Photo, C&OHS Coll., CSPR-10057.B01)

The division point dividing the New River and Kanawha mainline subdivisions is Handley, W. Va. Here in the early 1950s steam/diesel transition years we see GP9s ready to take loads west and a K-4 2-8-4 arriving eastbound with coal. In this region C&O coal flowed both east and west. (C&O Ry Photo, C&OHS Coll., CSPR-3402)

It was unusual to see the C&O's F7 units in coal fields service, but here two units have a loaded train of coal in tow at Ronda, W. Va. from mines in the Cabin Creek district in the early 1950s. (C&O Ry Photo, C&OHS Coll., CSPR-3403)

The Gauley Branch left the C&O main line at Gauley, (near the confluence of the Gauley and New Rivers forming the Kanawha) crossed over the river and then followed the Gauley River northward. It ultimately connected with the NYC and its side of the NF&G. Photos of operations on this branch are scarce. However, this June 1954 photo shows operations at the Belva Coal Company's mine at Belva. The large modern tipple apparently had a large capacity. A variety of C&O cars, including a re-sided composite hopper, are in evidence. Note the long conveyor in the foreground leading to a hopper for loading into highway trucks. The corrugated galvanized siding used on this type was perhaps the most common material seen on tipples. (C&O Ry Photo, C&OHS Coll., CSPR-10057.BB03)

C&O 70-ton 3-bay hopper No. 98615 seems to be loaded beyond capacity. The heap of pea coal seems well above the end extensions. Note the lump coal in the nearer car. The long conveyor brought coal down the hillside after the mine cars dumped it in the big shed-covered hopper. (C&O Ry Photo, C&OHS Coll., CSPR-10057.BB06)

The Coal River District branches off the main line at St,. Albans, W. Va., and consists of the Coal River and the Big Coal Subdivisions and a score of short branches. Here a C&O K-4 2-8-4 with empties headed for the Danville, W. Va. marshalling yard pauses at Sproul for water in July 1947. (Gene Huddleston photo, C&OHS Coll., COHS-1810)

This impressive tipple belonged to the Guyan Eagle Coal Company #5 mine at Kelly, W. Va. This mine was located on a short branch called the "Kelly Mine Extension" of the Coal River Subdivision. Of the common corrugated galvanized design, the tipple was at the very end of the line. The box car was probably delivering supplies of some kind. (C&O Ry Photo, C&OHS Coll., CSPR 10057.HH10)

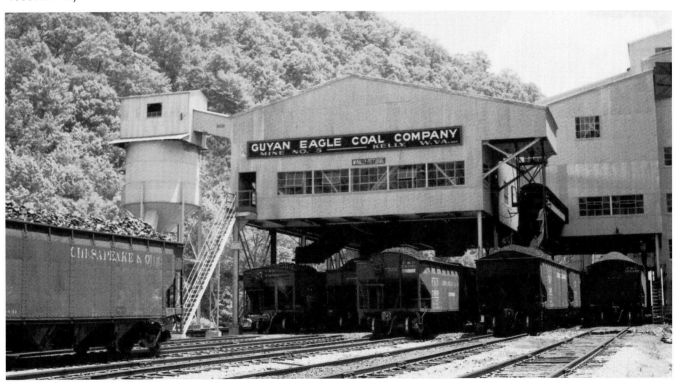

From the other end of the Kelly tipple we see the actual loading operation taking place in a variety of C&O offset side hopper cars. Fine slack is seen piled high in the car to the right. (C&O Ry Photo, C&OHS Coll., CSPR 10057.HH05

Between the two tipple structures we can see a C&O hopper being loaded by the conveyor being lowered into the car. A very large size of lump coal has been heaped into the car next to it. (C&O Ry Photo, C&OHS Coll., CSPR 10057.HH02)

The compact complex of buildings at Montcoal is evident here as a row of C&O hoppers of various types awaits loading. Note the car on its cables traveling back up the mountain, with the wire mesh netting below to catch any debris that might fall from these cars as they made the trip down and back. (C&O Ry Photo, C&OHS Coll., CSPR 10057.KK10)

The Marsh Fork Subdivision was located off the Big Coal Subdivision. Located five miles up this line was Montcoal where Armco Steel Corp. operated a mine, seen here in June 1954. At least three mine openings, high up the side of the hill are supplying coal to the tipple and cleaning plant, two by means of small cars on rails and one by suspended cable cars. The cylindrical silo in the foreground is for loading coal into highway trucks such as the one seen nearby. Note the chute. This was probably for slack grade coal. (C&O Ry Photo, C&OHS Coll., CSPR 10057.KK06)

Another view of the loading area at the Montcoal tipple shows hoppers being loaded. (C&O Ry Photo, C&OHS Coll., CSPR 10057.KK12)

An amazing complex and jumble of cable cars, netting, conveyors, and supports, surrounds the main tipple, at Montcoal (See previous pages) making this a very intricate design. (C&O Ry Photo, C&OHS Coll., CSPR 10057.KK09)

One mile further up the Marsh Fork branch was another Armco mine, at Stickney, W. Va. A much smaller and simpler operation than Montcoal, the tipple was supplied by a tramway leading up to the mine head. (C&O Ry Photo, C&OHS Coll., CSPR 10057.LL02).

The Seng Creek Subdivision connected the Big Coal Subdivision portion of the Coal River District with the Cabin Creek branch by way of a tunnel at the top of the ridge between the two watersheds. Here at Ameagle we see the American Eagle Colliery Company's tipple. Coal comes down the mountainside by tram at left and is processed inside the unusually tall tipple structure. The sign at the gable indicates that the tipple was built by Roberts & Schaeffer engineering. Other signs often see on the sides of tipples are "Fairmont," and "Link-Belt." (C&O Ry Photo, C&OHS Coll., CSPR 10057.LL6)

A side view gives a better appreciation for the massive nature of this unusual tipple, dwarfing the hoppers that are being loaded beneath it rather than at the end as in most facilities. (C&O Ry Photo, C&OHS Coll., CSPR 10057.LL4)

The Logan Subdivision was built just after the turn of the 20th Century to exploit the huge reserves in southwestern West Virginia. Peach Creek Yard at Logan served as the hub for this activity with at least a dozen branches from there tapping the rich coal seams. This scene was at Peach Creek in January 1946, filled with Mallets, smoke, and steam. (C&O Ry Photo, C&OHS Coll., CSPR-231)

Here H-4 2-6-6-2 Mallet No. 1331 has a mine shifter train of loads coming into Peach Creek about 1950. (Gene Huddleston photo, C&OH Coll., COHS-1124)

On the Rum Creek Subdivision in the Logan field, we see the Amherst Coal Company's MacGregor tipple at Slagle, W. Va. in June 1954. A modern plant with four tracks for car loading, the coal from the mine can be seen arriving in mine cars on the trestle at left. The C&O 50-ton hopper in the foreground is heaped in the traditional way. Other cars nearer the tipple are partially loaded. (C&O Ry Photo, C&OHS Coll., CSPR-10057.AA07)

Another view of the MacGregor tipple shows better the trestle for the mine cars feeding the coal to the plant. We wonder why the hopper in the foreground has been partially loaded only. (C&O Ry Photo, C&OHS Coll., CSPR-10057.AA12)

On the Buffalo Subdivision, the Guyan Eagle Coal Company's #1 mine at Amherstdale is again seen in June 1954. This tipple shows quite a bit of weathering. A hopper is being loaded, and a dump truck lettered for the coal company is receiving slate and refuse from the tipple to be carried away and dumped. (C&O Ry Photo, C&OHS Coll., CSPR-10057.CC01)

Stowe was another point on the coal-rich Buffalo subdivision, and the Guyan Eagle mine No. 4 is sending out neatly trimmed loads of rather large-lump coal at this small 3-track tipple in June 1954. (C&O Ry Photo, C&OHS Coll., CSPR-10057.CC06)

Another Amherst Coal Company mine at Braeholm on the Buffalo branch features a fairly small compact tipple receiving its coal from a steep tramway. The stone structure to the left is the power house. Most mines generated their own power, by this time electricity, and the powerhouse was generally built solidly of stone, brick, or block. (C&O Ry Photo, C&OHS Coll., CSPR-10057.BB12)

The other end of the Braeholm Amherst mine shows that all loading in this tipple is done beneath, whereas the more common method is by conveyor at the end of the building. Miners automobiles add to the scene. (C&O Ry Photo, C&OHS Coll., CSPR-10057.BB09)

The Elk Creek Subdivision served the Elk Creek Coal Company's tipple and preparation plant at Emmett, W. Va. A very modern looking facility, it is receiving its coal from a tram at right, and refuse is probably being shunted away through the covered conveyor at the left. A gondola and several hoppers are under the tipple for loading. (C&O Ry Photo, C&OHS Coll., CSPR-10057.DD11)

At ground level a mine car rider is maneuvering a string of hoppers toward the tipple for loading. (C&O Ry Photo, C&OHS Coll., CSPR-2106)

A more distant view of the Emmett facility shows two long cuts of loads ready for pickup with three different grades of coal. Note the company town to the left in the trees. (C&O Ry Photo, C&OHS Coll., CSPR-10057.DD10)

The Dorrance colliery tipple at Omar was a huge operation with conveyors in several directions, a large tipple building, as well as a yard jammed with empties ready to be loaded in 1948. (C&O Ry Photo, C&OHS Coll., CSPR-2107)

A close-up of one of the Dorrance mine's cars. (C&O Ry Photo, C&OHS Coll., CSPR-2115)

An overhead view at the Dorrance tipple. Loaded mine cars seem to be in the left tramway and empties in the right. (C&O Ry Photo, C&OHS Coll., CSPR-2109)

A general view shows the Dorrance Colliery tipple to be impressive for its complexity and size. It appears to have six tracks for loading. (C&O Ry Photo, C&OHS Coll., CSPR-10057.FF-06)

C&O's Kentucky coal reaches are along the Big Sandy River, which helps form the border with West Virginia. Operating out of yards at Paintsville, Martin, and Shelby, the area consists of at least 13 branches tapping coal seams. Here a train of loads is leaving Prestonsburg, Ky. bound for Russell about 1950 with K-4 No. 2716 for power. (C&O Ry Photo, C&OHS Coll., CSPR-2694)

This photo of the tipple at Evanston, Ky. (Dawkins Subdivision off the Big Sandy) belonging to the Princess Elkhorn Coal Company, is a perfect example of a coal mine scene, with the C&O mine run train moving along in the foreground and the tipple with its steep tram in the background, populated with hoppers. (C&O Ry Photo, C&OHS Coll., CSPR-3376)

One of the marshalling yards and engine terminals on the Big Sandy District was at Martin, Kentucky, seen here populated with Mallets and a switcher in late 1952. (D. Wallace Johnson Photo)

One of the very large tipples in the Big Sandy field was this Consolidation Coal Company operation at Jenkins, Kentucky, (Sandy Valley & Elkhorn Subdivision) seen here in 1944. It covers the valley with multiple conveyors sprouting from either side. The power house with its tall stack is clearly visible. The loaded yard is filled with gondolas with not a hopper car in sight. (C&O Ry Photo, C&OHS Coll., CSPR-136)

A close-up view of the Consolidation Coal tipple at Jenkins reveals a big logo-emblazoned sign above the loading area, not a common practice in the coal fields. Again, only gondolas are visible being loaded in this 1944 photo. (C&O Ry Photo, C&OHS Coll., CSPR-183)

A miner takes a sample of coal being loaded at the Consolidation Jenkins tipple. He will take the coal to the office where it will be checked to ensure its quality. (C&O Ry Photo, C&OHS Coll., CSPR-199)

The Republic Steel Corporation mine at tipple at Republic, Ky. in June 1954. The mine opening is at the top of the hill with a steep tram to the tipple. Hoppers for loading highway trucks are seen at left. This is on the Road Creek Subdivision of the Big Sandy district. (C&O Ry Photo, C&OHS Coll., CSPR-10057.035)

One is reminded of the "machine in the garden" ideal in looking at this general view of the Clinchfield Coal Corp. mine at Meade, Virginia, in June 1954. It is a large and complex facility with the usual conveyors and trams, yard for empties at left, and for loads in the distance at right. Large squat water tanks are on the hill at left. C&O had only one line which served coal mines in the state of Virginia, and that was the Meade Fork branch off the big Sandy line. Built in 1948, this was the last big coal field branch construction on the C&O. (C&O Ry Photo, C&OHS Coll., CSPR-10057.071)

A close view of the loading side of the Meade tipple shows huge mine-run lumps falling into the car at left, large lump next, then stove size, and finally the pea grade at right. (C&O Ry Photo, C&OHS Coll., CSPR-2667)

The empty yard provides a good perspective on the loading operation at the Price plant. This photo inspired C&O artist to do the painting used on the cover of this book. (C&O Ry Photo, C&OHS Coll., CSPR-2679)

The Big Sandy's Long Fork Subdivision was the location of Island Creek Coal Company's preparation plant at Price, Kentucky. Pictures of this huge and ultramodern facility were used by C&O in countless brochures, calendars, and advertisements. This one in particular showing the loaded C&O hoppers in the foreground, was a favorite. The empty yard tracks are in the distance, filed with cars. This plant had a huge capacity. (C&O Ry Photo, C&OHS Coll., CSPR-3378)

A closer view of the Price tipple, with loads in C&O cars of various heritage. (C&O Ry Photo, C&OHS Coll., CSPR-3378)

KAYMOOR COAL MINE - 1900
FAYETTEVILLE VICINITY   WEST VIRGINIA

LOCATED ON THE PRECIPITOUS SLOPE OF THE NEW RIVER GORGE, IN THE HEART OF WEST VIRGINIA'S FAMOUS "SMOKELESS COAL FIELD", KAYMOOR COAL MINE OPERATED FROM 1900 TO 1962, PRODUCING APPROXIMATELY 17,000,000 TONS OF COAL. NAMED FOR JAMES KAY, WHO OVERSAW CONSTRUCTION, KAYMOOR WAS ORIGINALLY A CAPTIVE MINE OPENED BY THE LOW MOOR IRON COMPANY TO PROVIDE COKE FOR ITS HOT BLAST IRON FURNACES 100 MILES EAST IN THE COVINGTON, VIRGINIA IRON REGION. THE SEWELL SEAM OF THE NEW RIVER GORGE, INTO WHICH KAYMOOR'S 10 FOOT DRIFT OPENING WAS DRIVEN, CONTAINED LOW VOLATILE BITUMINOUS COAL (HENCE THE NAME "SMOKELESS") WHICH PRODUCED THE BEST BLAST FURNACE COKE IN THE COUNTRY. BUT THE ELEVATION OF THE SEAM, 560 FEET ABOVE THE FLOOR OF THE GORGE AND THE TRACKS OF THE CHESAPEAKE AND OHIO RAILWAY, POSED SPECIAL ENGINEERING CHALLENGES, TO MOVE MEN AND EQUIPMENT FROM COMPANY TOWNS AT BOTH THE TOP AND BOTTOM OF THE GORGE TO THE DRIFT OPENING, A "MOUNTAIN HAULAGE", A SINGLE TRACK INCLINE WITH A STEAM POWERED CABLE HOISTING DRUM, WAS BUILT. TO QUICKLY AND SAFELY LOWER COAL TO THE PROCESSING PLANT AND BEEHIVE COKE OVENS AT THE FLOOR OF THE GORGE, A TWO TRACK GRAVITY INCLINE WAS INSTALLED. WITH FEW MODIFICATIONS, BOTH SYSTEMS REMAINED IN SERVICE THROUGHOUT KAYMOOR'S 62 YEARS OF OPERATION.

AS THE ERA OF THE BEEHIVE COKE OVEN AND THE MERCHANT PIG IRON INDUSTRY WANED, SO DID THE FORTUNES OF LOW MOOR. WHEN ITS TIPPLE BURNED IN 1924, KAYMOOR WAS SOLD TO THE NEW RIVER AND POCAHONTAS CONSOLIDATED COAL COMPANY, A SUBSIDIARY OF BERWIND-WHITE CORP. OF PHILADELPHIA. BERWIND INSTALLED A NEW PROCESSING PLANT IN 1925 AND A SIMON-CARVES BAUM JIG WASHER AROUND 1928, BOTH BUILT BY LINK BELT CO. OF CHICAGO.

KAYMOOR IS A SIGNIFICANT INDUSTRIAL ARCHEOLOGICAL SITE FOR SEVERAL REASONS. ITS HEADHOUSE AND INCLINE SYSTEMS ILLUSTRATE THE SPECIAL TECHNIQUES EMPLOYED BY EARLY 20TH CENTURY AMERICAN MINERS TO WREST COAL FROM OUTCROPS ON STEEP SLOPES. ITS BAUM JIG WASHER, PATENTED BY SIMON-CARVES OF ENGLAND, IS EVIDENCE OF THE MAJOR TRANSITION TO THE PRODUCTION OF WASHED COAL THAT BEGAN IN THE UNITED STATES IN THE LATE 1920'S. ITS FAN HOUSES, POWER HOUSE, DRIFT OPENINGS, AND OTHER INTEGRAL ELEMENTS SURVIVE, PROVIDING EXAMPLES OF TYPICAL MINING PRACTICE OF THE ERA.

THE KAYMOOR COAL MINE RECORDING PROJECT WAS UNDERTAKEN BY THE HISTORIC AMERICAN ENGINEERING RECORD (HAER), AN AGENCY OF THE NATIONAL PARK SERVICE, U.S. DEPARTMENT OF THE INTERIOR, DURING THE SUMMER OF 1986. THE PROJECT WAS CO-SPONSORED BY THE NEW RIVER GORGE NATIONAL RIVER, OAK HILL, WEST VIRGINIA, JIM CARRICO, SUPERINTENDENT, AND THE HISTORIC AMERICAN BUILDINGS SURVEY / HISTORIC AMERICAN ENGINEERING RECORD (HABS/HAER), ROBERT J. KAPSCH, CHIEF. THE FIELD TEAM, UNDER THE DIRECTION OF ERIC DE LONY, PRINCIPAL ARCHITECT, HAER, CONSISTED OF DONALD KRAFT, PROJECT CO-SUPERVISOR AND ENGINEER (COLUMBIA UNIVERSITY), JACK BERGSTRESSER, PROJECT CO-SUPERVISOR AND HISTORIAN (AUBURN UNIVERSITY), ARCHITECTURAL TECHNICIANS MABEL A. BAIGES (KANSAS STATE UNIVERSITY), BENITA C. WELCH (UNIVERSITY OF ILLINOIS), AND MICHAEL P. O'BOYLE (US/ICOMOS AND UNIVERSITY COLLEGE, DUBLIN, IRELAND), AND GRAPHIC DESIGNER RICHARD SARUN (CLEVELAND INSTITUTE OF ART). FORMAL ON-SITE PHOTOGRAPHY WAS DONE BY JET LOWE, HAER STAFF PHOTOGRAPHER. SPECIAL CONSULTING SERVICES WERE PROVIDED BY JOHN R. BOWIE, AIA (WALLINGFORD, PA.).

LOCATION MAP TAKEN FROM USGS 7.5' SERIES FAYETTEVILLE QUADRANGLE (PHOTOREVISED 1976). UTM LOCATIONS:
17.494190, 4210890 (HEADHOUSE)
17.494460, 4211020 (PROCESSING PLANT)

SITE PLAN FROM "INSURANCE MAP OF KAYMOOR Nº 1", PREPARED FOR NEW RIVER AND POCAHONTAS CONSOLIDATED COAL CO., KAYMOOR DIVISION, 1926. (FROM BERWIND-WHITE LAND COMPANY, CHARLESTON, WEST VIRGINIA)

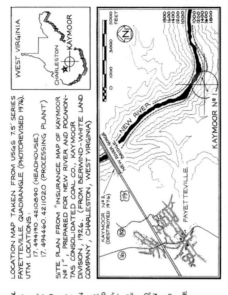

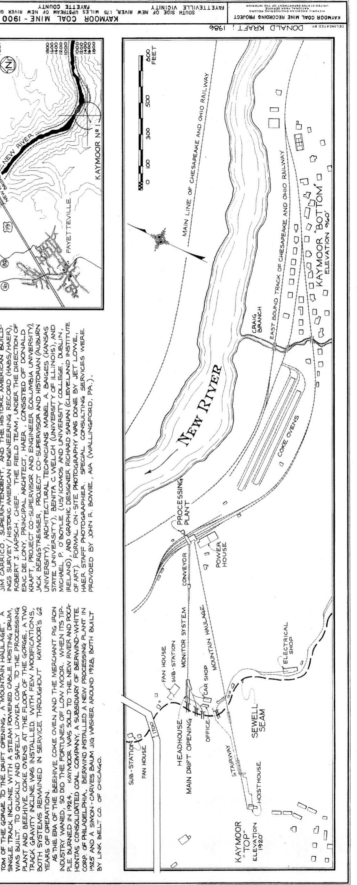

The Historic American Engineering Record and Historical American Buildings Survey are a part of the U. S. National Park Service, and record industrial and architectural sites that have been preserved or which were about to be demolished but are of historical importance as prime examples of a particular style or process. Detailed surveys and historical research as well as archeology were used to reconstruct how the Kaymoor Mine operated between 1900 and 1962. The entire process of a typical drift mine is shown. Full size (24"x36" approximately) drawings are available from COHS. Visit www.chessieshop.com or call 800-453-COHS for details.

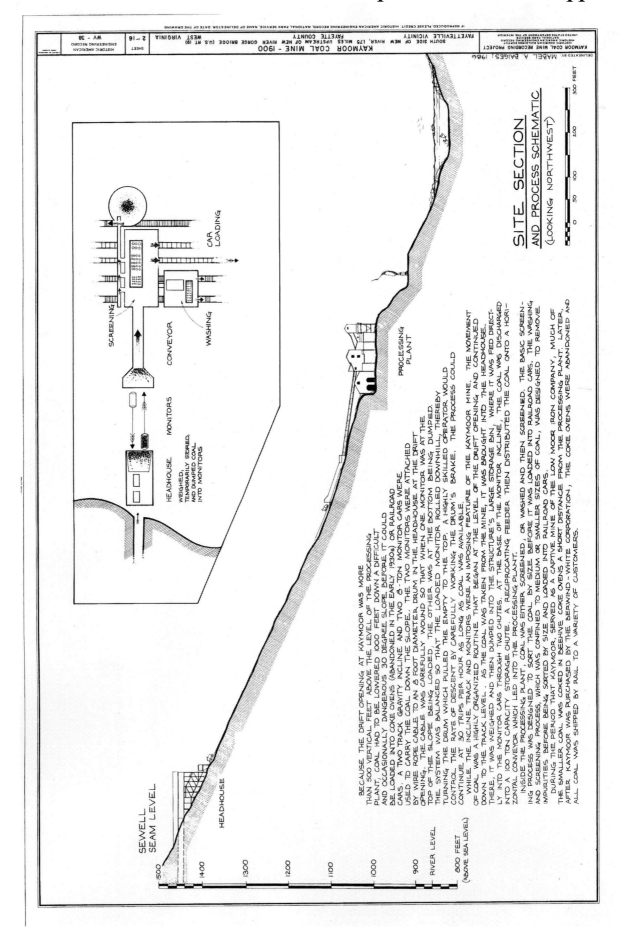

→ STAIRWAY TO KAYMOOR TOP

SUPERINTENDENT'S OFFICE

NOTE

TRACK LOCATION BASED ON ORAL INTERVIEWS WITH PAST EMPLOYEES, HISTORICAL PHOTOGRAPHS FROM THE NPS COLLECTION, AND ON-SITE EVIDENCE.

UP TO KAYMOOR TOP

LAMP HOUSE

BENCH LEVEL SITE PLAN

SITE KEY

VENTILATION OPENING

OPENING FOR ELECTRICAL SERVICE

VENTILATION FAN UNIT

MINE DRAINAGE

CONCRETE PAD FOR ELECTRICAL SUBSTATION (NOW REMOVED)

SAND HOPPER

MAIN DRIFT OPENING

FAN HOUSE COMPLEX

BUILT BY BERWIND AFTER 1928

2000'

CAR REPAIR SHOP

FORMER VENTILATION OPENINGS

MOUNTAIN HAULAGE

TO MOVE PEOPLE AND MATERIALS

VENTILATION OPENING

FAN UNIT PEDESTALS

SIROCCO VENTILATING FAN, BY AMERICAN BLOWER CO. (DETROIT) IN OPERATION 1909 - 1922 8'-4" DIAMETER, DOUBLE INLET ELECTRICALLY POWERED GENERALLY RUN AT ABOUT 150 RPM

POWDER HOUSE

ELECTRICAL SUBSTATION (PARTIALLY DEMOLISHED)

DOWN TO KAYMOOR BOTTOM

BENCH LEVEL SITE PLAN

SCALE: 1" = 20'-0"

FAN HOUSE COMPLEX

BUILT BY LOW MOOR, 1919

ELECTRICAL REPAIR SHOP

250'

HEADHOUSE

0 10 20   50   100 FEET

0   5   10   20   30 METERS

THE MOVEMENT OF MEN, COAL CARS, AND MINE LOCOMOTIVES ALONG THE BENCH AT THE DRIFT OPENINGS, 560 FEET ABOVE THE FLOOR OF THE GORGE, WAS A COMPLICATED PROCESS PERFORMED IN A NARROW AREA. MINERS WERE SHUTTLED TO THE BENCH FROM COMPANY TOWNS AT THE TOP AND BOTTOM OF THE GORGE VIA THE "MOUN-TAIN HAULAGE" (1), A SINGLE TRACK INCLINE POWERED BY A HOISTING ENGINE AND CABLE DRUM AT THE TOP OF THE GORGE. THE MINERS MOVED FROM THE HAULAGE DROP-OFF POINT (2), NEAR THE DRIFT OPENING, TO THE LAMPHOUSE (3), WHERE THEY PICKED UP THEIR LAMPS AND OTHER EQUIPMENT. THEY THEN ENTERED A WAITING ROOM JUST INSIDE THE DRIFT OPENING (4), AND AWAITED A MINE LOCO-MOTIVE PULLING EMPTY CARS THAT WOULD TRANSPORT THEM TO THEIR WORK PLACES DEEP WITHIN THE MINE.

ONCE AT WORK IN ROOMS ON EITHER SIDE OF THE MAIN LOCO-MOTIVE TRACK, MINERS BEGAN LOADING CARS EITHER WITH COAL OR SHALE. WHEN LOADED, THESE CARS WERE HAULED TO THE MAIN LOCOMOTIVE TRACK TO BE TRANSPORTED OUT OF THE MINE. DURING KAYMOOR'S EARLY YEARS, MULES PERFORMED THIS INTER-MEDIATE HAULAGE, BUT THEY SOON WERE REPLACED BY GATHERING LOCOMOTIVES, SMALLER VERSIONS OF THE ELECTRIC LOCOMOTIVES THAT TRAVELED IN AND OUT OF THE MINE.

ONCE A MAIN HAULAGE LOCOMOTIVE HAD PICKED UP A FULL STRING OF COAL CARS AND "SLATE" CARS (COAL CARS FILLED WITH SHALE), IT PROCEEDED TO THE SURFACE. AT THE DRIFT OPENING, THE LOCOMOTIVE, COAL CARS, AND SLATE CARS DIVERGED AND FOLLOWED ONE OF THREE SEPARATE TRACKS. THE LOCOMOTIVE STOPPED MOMENTARILY TO ALLOW A "SCOTCH MAN" (5) TO DISCONNECT THE STRING OF MINE CARS. IT THEN SWITCHED OFF THE MAIN TRACK, PROCEEDED ONTO A SIDING IN THE HEADHOUSE (6), REVERSED ITS MOTOR, AND RE-ENTERED THE MINE THROUGH A SEPARATE LOCOMOTIVE OPENING (7). IF THE LOCOMOTIVE NEEDED REPAIRS, IT COULD PROCEED A FEW HUNDRED FEET INTO THE MINE, SWITCH OVER TO ANOTHER TRACK, REVERSE ITS MOTOR, AND EXIT THROUGH A THIRD MINE OPENING, THE LOCOMOTIVE REPAIR EXIT (8), TO THE ELECTRICAL SHOP (9). GATHERING LOCOMOTIVES NEEDING REPAIR USED THE SAME EXIT. IF REPAIRS WERE NOT NECESSARY, THE MAIN HAULAGE LOCOMOTIVE WOULD PICK UP ANY EMPTY SLATE CARS THAT MIGHT BE WAITING ON THEIR SEPARATE TRACK (10) OUTSIDE THE MINE NEAR THE LOCOMOTIVE RETURN OPENING. IMMEDIATELY INSIDE THE MINE, THE LOCOMOTIVE PICKED UP ANY WAITING EMPTY COAL CARS THAT HAD BEEN BROUGHT BACK INTO THE MINE THROUGH A FOURTH OPENING, THE EMPTY COAL CAR ENTRANCE (11).

THE COAL AND SLATE CARS THAT HAD BEEN DETACHED FROM THE LOCOMOTIVE AT THE MAIN DRIFT OPENING WERE RELEASED INDIVID-UALLY ONTO ONE OF TWO TRACKS. THE COAL CARS WERE ALLOWED TO ROLL DOWN A SLIGHT GRADE INTO THE HEADHOUSE, WHERE THEY WERE STOPPED, WEIGHED, AND DUMPED. THEY WERE THEN SWITCHED BACK ONTO ANOTHER TRACK IN THE HEADHOUSE (12), WHERE THEY WERE ENGAGED ONTO WHAT THE MINERS REFERRED TO AS A CREEPER (13). THIS CHAIN MECHANISM SNAGGED THE CARS AND PULLED THEM BACK INTO THE MINE THROUGH THE EMPTY COAL CAR ENTRANCE.

THE SLATE CARS WERE SWITCHED BY THE SCOTCH MAN ONTO A SEPARATE TRACK (14) AND ROLLED DOWNHILL AROUND THE NORTH SIDE OF THE BENCH. THEY WERE THEN CONNECTED TO A CABLE AND PULLED TO THE TOP OF THE GORGE BY AN ENGINE DRIVEN HOISTING DRUM. AFTER BEING DUMPED WELL AWAY FROM THE SLOPE, THE CARS RETURNED TO THE BENCH LEVEL, PASSED UNDER THE SCALES IN THE HEADHOUSE, AND CAME TO A STOP. THEY WERE THEN READY TO BE HAULED BACK INTO THE MINE BY THE MAIN HAULAGE LOCOMOTIVE VIA THE LOCOMOTIVE-RETURN OPENING. IF REPAIRS WERE NECESSARY, BOTH THE COAL AND SLATE CARS COULD BE SWITCHED ONTO TRACKS THAT LED INTO THE CAR REPAIR SHOP (15).

HISTORIC AMERICAN ENGINEERING RECORD WV - 38

SHEET 3 "16

HISTORIC AMERICAN ENGINEERING RECORD NATIONAL PARK SERVICE, NAME OF DELINEATOR, DATE OF THE DRAWING

IF REPRODUCED, PLEASE CREDIT

KAYMOOR COAL MINE - 1900

SOUTH SIDE OF NEW RIVER, 175 MILES UPSTREAM OF NEW RIVER GORGE BRIDGE (U.S. RT. 19) WEST VIRGINIA

FAYETTEVILLE VICINITY   FAYETTE COUNTY

DONALD KRAFT, 1986

DELINEATED BY:

KAYMOOR COAL MINE RECORDING PROJECT

HISTORIC AMERICAN ENGINEERING RECORD UNITED STATES DEPARTMENT OF THE INTERIOR

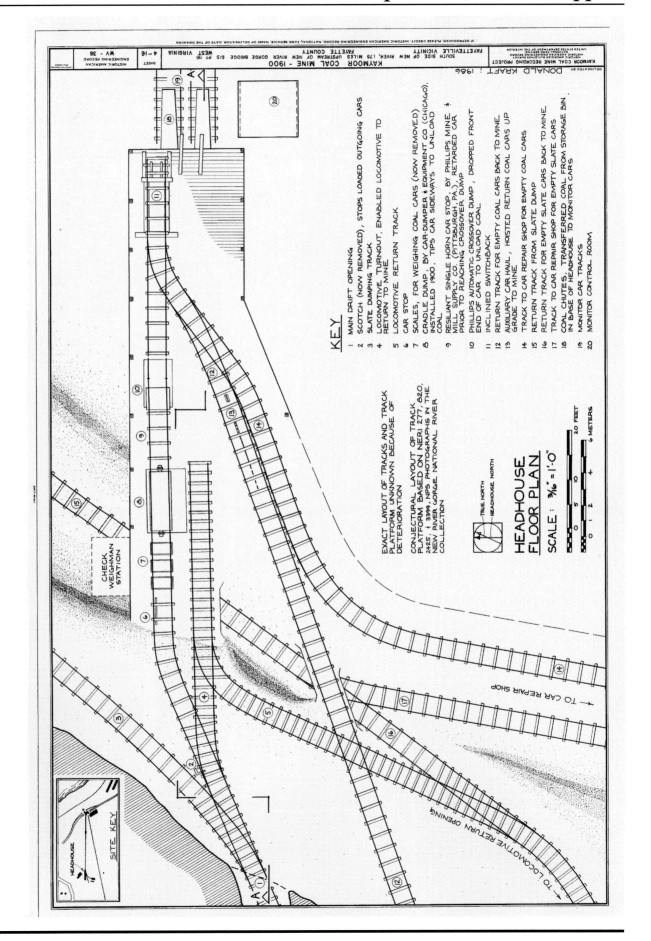

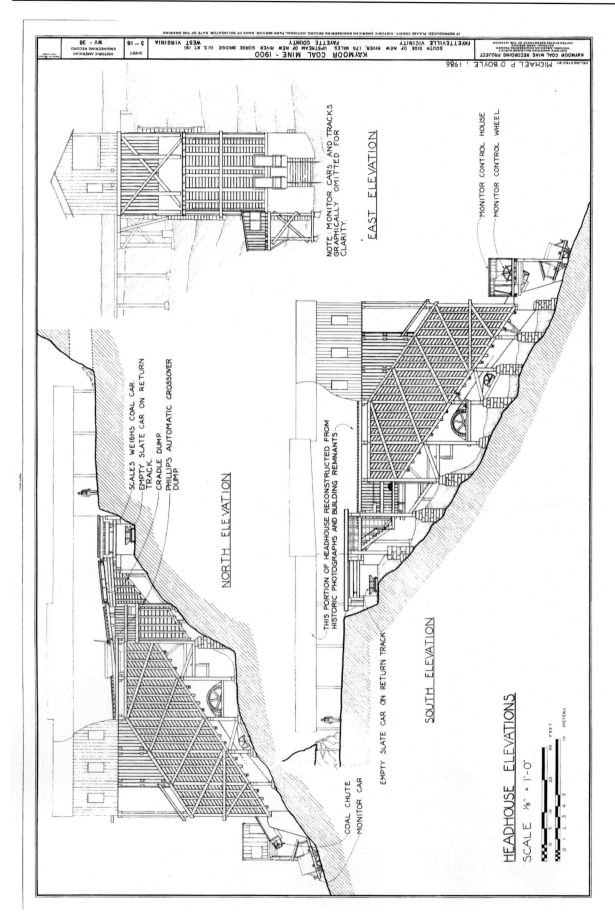

For information on purchasing reproductions of any of the photos or drawings in this book contact the Chesapeake & Ohio Historical Society Archives
312 East Ridgeway Street - Clifton Forge, VA - 24422 - 540-862-2210 or email cohs@cohs.org

KAYMOOR COAL MINE - 1900

SOUTH SIDE OF NEW RIVER, 1.75 MILES UPSTREAM OF NEW RIVER GORGE BRIDGE (U.S. RT 19)
FAYETTEVILLE VICINITY · FAYETTE COUNTY · WEST VIRGINIA

HISTORIC AMERICAN ENGINEERING RECORD — WV - 38 — SHEET 6 OF 16

DELINEATED BY MICHAEL P.O. BOYLE : 1986

THIS PORTION OF HEADHOUSE RECONSTRUCTED FROM HISTORIC PHOTOGRAPHS AND BUILDING REMNANTS

HEADHOUSE SECTION A-A
(LOOKING NORTH)

SCALE 5/16" = 1'-0"

KEY
1. MAIN DRIFT OPENING
2. APPROXIMATE LOCATION OF SCOTCH (NOW REMOVED):STOPS LOADED OUTGOING CAR
3. APPROXIMATE LOCATION OF CAR STOP
4. SCALES : WEIGHS COAL CAR
5. APPROXIMATE LOCATION OF EMPTY SLATE CAR RETURN TRACK
6. CRADLE DUMP (BY CAR DUMPER AND EQUIPMENT CO. CHICAGO, ILL.):TIPS CAR SIDEWAYS TO DUMP COAL.
7. CRADLE DUMP CHUTE
8. APRON CONVEYOR : FEEDS INTO MAIN STORAGE BIN
9. DISPOSAL CHUTE FOR COAL CONTAINING UNACCEPTABLE LEVELS OF SLATE
10. PHILLIPS RESILIENT SINGLE HORN CAR STOP (BY PHILLIPS MINE AND MILL SUPPLY CO. PITTSBURGH PA) RETARDS CAR PRIOR TO REACHING CROSSOVER DUMP.
11. PHILLIPS AUTOMATIC CROSSOVER DUMP: DROPS FRONT END OF CAR TO UNLOAD COAL
12. COUNTER WEIGHT FOR CROSSOVER DUMP
13. CROSSOVER DUMP CHUTE
14. RECIPROCATING FEEDER
15. INCLINED SWITCH BACK FOR EMPTY COAL CARS
16. MAIN STORAGE BIN
17. MAIN STORAGE BIN
18. COAL CHUTE: TRANSFERS COAL FROM MAIN STORAGE BIN TO MONITOR CARS
19. WOOD-LAPPED MONITOR CABLE DRUM
20. SHEAVE FOR MONITOR CABLE
21. MONITOR CAR

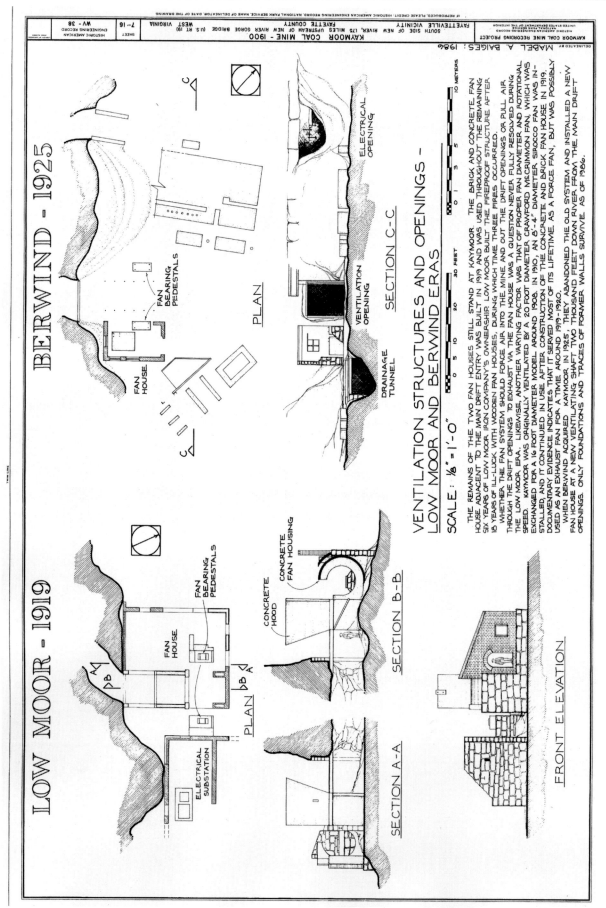

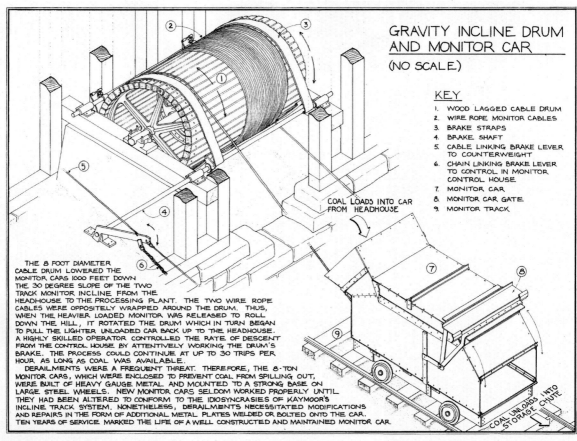

GRAVITY INCLINE DRUM
AND MONITOR CAR
(NO SCALE)

KEY
1. WOOD LAGGED CABLE DRUM
2. WIRE ROPE MONITOR CABLES
3. BRAKE STRAPS
4. BRAKE SHAFT
5. CABLE LINKING BRAKE LEVER TO COUNTERWEIGHT
6. CHAIN LINKING BRAKE LEVER TO CONTROL IN MONITOR CONTROL HOUSE.
7. MONITOR CAR
8. MONITOR CAR GATE
9. MONITOR TRACK

COAL LOADS INTO CAR FROM HEADHOUSE

COAL UNLOADS INTO STORAGE CHUTE

THE 8 FOOT DIAMETER CABLE DRUM LOWERED THE MONITOR CARS 1000 FEET DOWN THE 30 DEGREE SLOPE OF THE TWO TRACK MONITOR INCLINE FROM THE HEADHOUSE TO THE PROCESSING PLANT. THE TWO WIRE ROPE CABLES WERE OPPOSITELY WRAPPED AROUND THE DRUM. THUS, WHEN THE HEAVIER LOADED MONITOR WAS RELEASED TO ROLL DOWN THE HILL, IT ROTATED THE DRUM WHICH IN TURN BEGAN TO PULL THE LIGHTER UNLOADED CAR BACK UP TO THE HEADHOUSE. A HIGHLY SKILLED OPERATOR CONTROLLED THE RATE OF DESCENT FROM THE CONTROL HOUSE BY ATTENTIVELY WORKING THE DRUM'S BRAKE. THE PROCESS COULD CONTINUE AT UP TO 30 TRIPS PER HOUR, AS LONG AS COAL WAS AVAILABLE.

DERAILMENTS WERE A FREQUENT THREAT. THEREFORE, THE 8-TON MONITOR CARS, WHICH WERE ENCLOSED TO PREVENT COAL FROM SPILLING OUT, WERE BUILT OF HEAVY GAUGE METAL AND MOUNTED TO A STRONG BASE ON LARGE STEEL WHEELS. NEW MONITOR CARS SELDOM WORKED PROPERLY UNTIL THEY HAD BEEN ALTERED TO CONFORM TO THE IDIOSYNCRASIES OF KAYMOOR'S INCLINE TRACK SYSTEM. NONETHELESS, DERAILMENTS NECESSITATED MODIFICATIONS AND REPAIRS IN THE FORM OF ADDITIONAL METAL PLATES WELDED OR BOLTED ONTO THE CAR. TEN YEARS OF SERVICE MARKED THE LIFE OF A WELL CONSTRUCTED AND MAINTAINED MONITOR CAR.

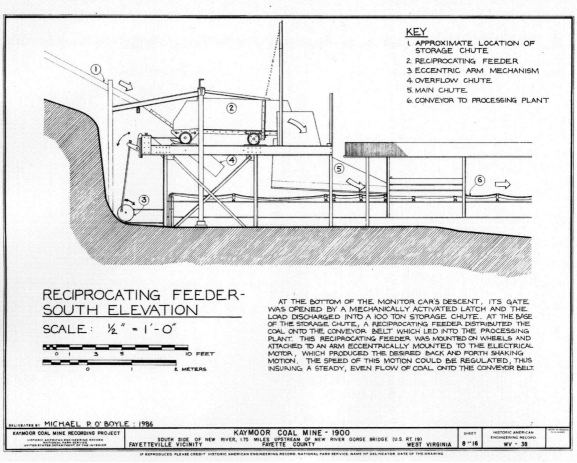

KEY
1. APPROXIMATE LOCATION OF STORAGE CHUTE
2. RECIPROCATING FEEDER
3. ECCENTRIC ARM MECHANISM
4. OVERFLOW CHUTE
5. MAIN CHUTE
6. CONVEYOR TO PROCESSING PLANT

RECIPROCATING FEEDER-
SOUTH ELEVATION
SCALE: ½" = 1'-0"

AT THE BOTTOM OF THE MONITOR CAR'S DESCENT, ITS GATE WAS OPENED BY A MECHANICALLY ACTIVATED LATCH AND THE LOAD DISCHARGED INTO A 100 TON STORAGE CHUTE. AT THE BASE OF THE STORAGE CHUTE, A RECIPROCATING FEEDER DISTRIBUTED THE COAL ONTO THE CONVEYOR BELT WHICH LED INTO THE PROCESSING PLANT. THIS RECIPROCATING FEEDER WAS MOUNTED ON WHEELS AND ATTACHED TO AN ARM ECCENTRICALLY MOUNTED TO THE ELECTRICAL MOTOR, WHICH PRODUCED THE DESIRED BACK AND FORTH SHAKING MOTION. THE SPEED OF THIS MOTION COULD BE REGULATED, THUS INSURING A STEADY, EVEN FLOW OF COAL ONTO THE CONVEYOR BELT.

DELINEATED BY MICHAEL P. O'BOYLE : 1986

KAYMOOR COAL MINE RECORDING PROJECT
HISTORIC AMERICAN ENGINEERING RECORD
NATIONAL PARK SERVICE
UNITED STATES DEPARTMENT OF THE INTERIOR

KAYMOOR COAL MINE - 1900
SOUTH SIDE OF NEW RIVER, 1.75 MILES UPSTREAM OF NEW RIVER GORGE BRIDGE (U.S. RT. 19)
FAYETTEVILLE VICINITY   FAYETTE COUNTY   WEST VIRGINIA

SHEET 8 OF 16

HISTORIC AMERICAN ENGINEERING RECORD
WV - 38

IF REPRODUCED, PLEASE CREDIT HISTORIC AMERICAN ENGINEERING RECORD, NATIONAL PARK SERVICE, NAME OF DELINEATOR, DATE OF THE DRAWING

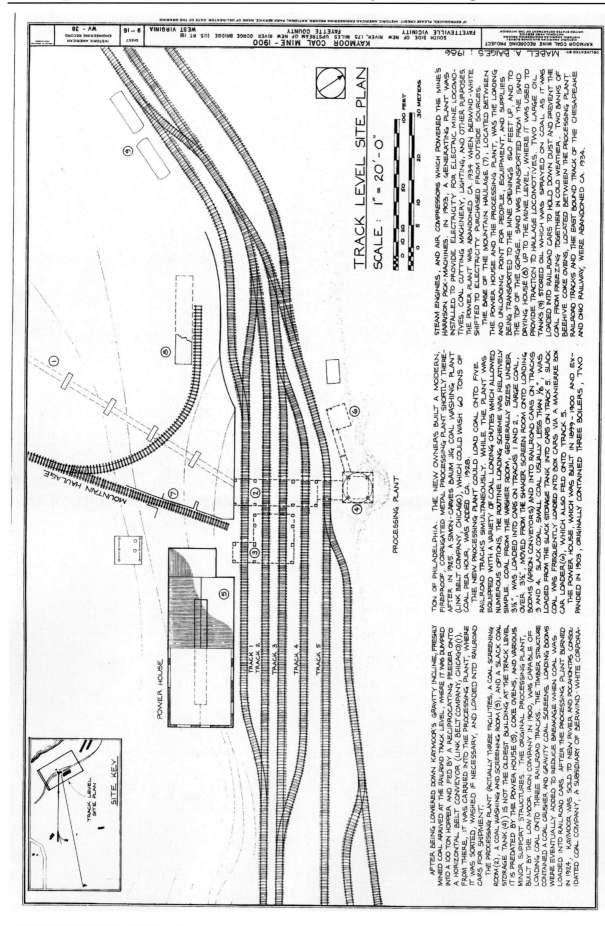

For information on purchacing reproductions of any of the photos or drawings in this book contact the Chesapeake & Ohio Historical Society Archives
312 East Ridgeway Street - Clifton Forge, VA - 24422 - 540-862-2210 or email cohs@cohs.org

PROCESSING PLANT ELEVATIONS

SCALE: 1/8" = 1'-0"

NORTH ELEVATION

SCREENING HOUSE

SLACK COAL STORAGE TANK

SOUTH ELEVATION

WASH HOUSE

LOADING BOOM (TYP)

SLACK COAL STORAGE TANK

EAST (RIVER) ELEVATION

WASH HOUSE

(FORMER) POWERHOUSE

SLACK COAL STORAGE TANK

SLACK COAL CONVEYOR

MANIERRE BOX CAR LOADER

DELINEATED BY MABEL A. BAIGES

KAYMOOR COAL MINE RECORDING PROJECT
HISTORIC AMERICAN ENGINEERING RECORD
NATIONAL PARK SERVICE
HISTORIC AMERICAN BUILDINGS SURVEY
UNITED STATES DEPARTMENT OF THE INTERIOR

KAYMOOR COAL MINE - 1900
SOUTH SIDE OF NEW RIVER, 1.75 MILES UPSTREAM OF NEW RIVER GORGE BRIDGE (U.S. RT. 19)
FAYETTEVILLE VICINITY   FAYETTE COUNTY   WEST VIRGINIA

HISTORIC AMERICAN ENGINEERING RECORD

WV - 38

SHEET 10 OF 16

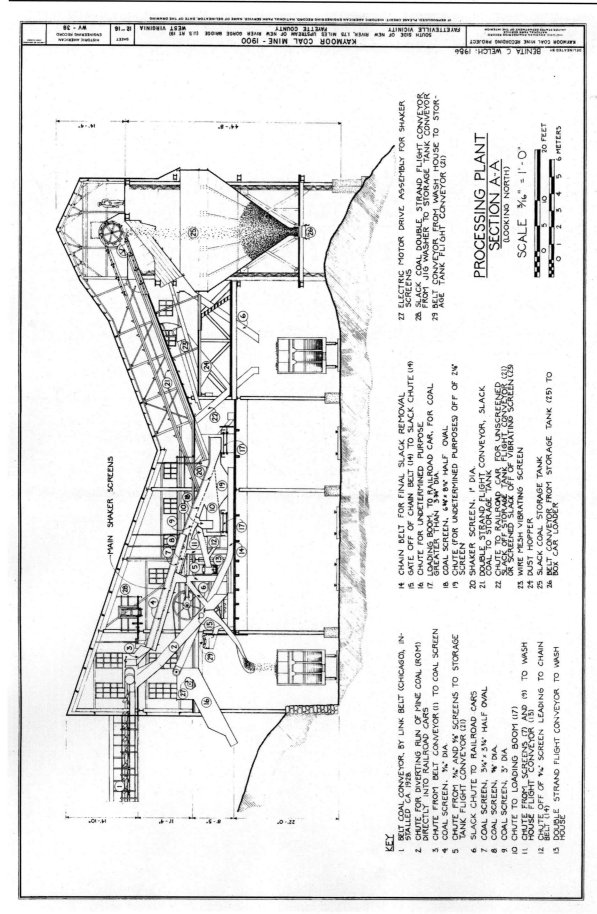

KAYMOOR COAL MINE - 1900

SOUTH SIDE OF NEW RIVER, 1.75 MILES UPSTREAM OF NEW RIVER GORGE BRIDGE (US RT 19)

FAYETTEVILLE VICINITY   FAYETTE COUNTY   WEST VIRGINIA

HISTORIC AMERICAN ENGINEERING RECORD   SHEET 13 of 16   WV - 38

UNITED STATES DEPARTMENT OF THE INTERIOR
NATIONAL PARK SERVICE
HISTORIC AMERICAN ENGINEERING RECORD
KAYMOOR COAL MINE RECORDING PROJECT

DELINEATED BY: BENITA C. WELCH, 1986

SECTION C-C
THROUGH COAL WASHING ROOM
(LOOKING NORTH)

SECTION B-B
THROUGH MAIN SCREENING ROOM
AND COAL WASHING ROOM
(LOOKING EAST)

KEY

1. MAIN SHAKER SCREEN
2. CHUTE OFF OF 5/8" SHAKER SCREEN LEADING TO SLACK TANK FLIGHT CONVEYOR (5)
3. DOUBLE STRAND FLIGHT CONVEYOR, SLACK COAL TO STORAGE TANK
4. CHUTE OFF OF 5" SHAKER SCREEN TO WASH HOUSE FLIGHT CONVEYOR (6)
5. LOADING BOOM, TO RAILROAD CAR, FOR COAL GREATER THAN 3¼"
6. DOUBLE STRAND FLIGHT CONVEYOR TO WASH HOUSE
7. CHUTE FROM WASH HOUSE FLIGHT CONVEYOR (6) TO JIG WASH (8)
8. SIMON - CARVES BAUM TYPE JIG WASHER
9. REFUSE DEWATERING CONVEYOR
10. WASHERY RESERVOIR
11. HOIST
12. COAL SCREEN, ¼" DIA.
13. COAL SCREEN, 1⅛" x 2" HALF OVAL
14. COAL SCREEN, ¾" DIA.
15. CHUTE FROM SHAKER SCREENS TO LOWER LEVEL
16. CHAIN CONVEYOR TO RAILROAD CARS
17. COAL CRUSHER
18. DEWATERING SCREEN
19. REFUSE CHUTE
20. CHAIN CONVEYOR TO TRANSPORT REFUSE

SCALE ³⁄₁₆" = 1'-0"

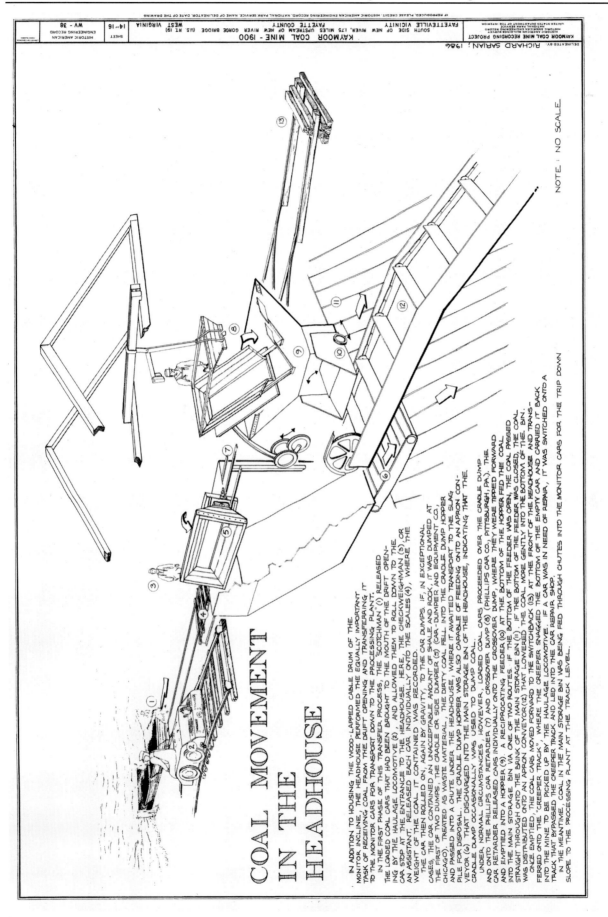

COAL MOVEMENT IN THE HEADHOUSE

KAYMOOR COAL MINE - 1900

SOUTH SIDE OF NEW RIVER, 175 MILES UPSTREAM OF NEW RIVER GORGE BRIDGE (US RT 19)
FAYETTEVILLE VICINITY   FAYETTE COUNTY   WEST VIRGINIA

KAYMOOR COAL MINE RECORDING PROJECT

DELINEATED BY: RICHARD SARIAN; 1986

NOTE : NO SCALE

IN ADDITION TO HOUSING THE WOOD-LAPPED CABLE DRUM OF THE MONITOR INCLINE, THE HEADHOUSE PERFORMED THE EQUALLY IMPORTANT TASK OF RECEIVING COAL FROM THE DRIFT OPENING AND TRANSFERRING IT TO THE MONITOR CARS FOR TRANSPORT DOWN TO THE PROCESSING PLANT.

IN THE FIRST PHASE OF THIS TRANSFER PROCESS, THE "SCOTCHMAN" (1) RELEASED THE LOADED COAL CARS THAT HAD BEEN BROUGHT TO THE MOUTH OF THE DRIFT OPENING BY THE HAULAGE LOCOMOTIVE (2), AND ALLOWED THEM TO ROLL DOWN TO THE CAR STOP AT THE ENTRANCE TO THE HEADHOUSE. HERE THE CHECKWEIGHMAN (3), OR AN ASSISTANT, RELEASED EACH CAR INDIVIDUALLY ONTO THE SCALES (4), WHERE THE WEIGHT OF THE COAL IT CONTAINED WAS RECORDED.

THE CAR THEN ROLLED ON, AGAIN BY GRAVITY, TO THE CAR DUMPS. IF, IN EXCEPTIONAL CASES, THE CAR CONTAINED AN UNACCEPTABLE AMOUNT OF SHALE AND ROCK, IT WAS DUMPED AT THE FIRST OF TWO DUMPS, THE CRADLE OR SIDE DUMPER (5) (CAR-DUMPER AND EQUIPMENT CO, CHICAGO). TREATED AS WASTE MATERIAL, THE DIRTY COAL FELL INTO THE CRADLE DUMP HOPPER AND PASSED INTO A CHUTE UNDER THE HEADHOUSE, WHERE IT AWAITED TRANSPORT TO THE SLAG PILE FOR DISPOSAL. THE CRADLE DUMP HOPPER WAS ALSO CAPABLE OF FEEDING ONTO AN APRON CONVEYOR (6) THAT DISCHARGED INTO THE MAIN STORAGE BIN OF THE HEADHOUSE, INDICATING THAT THE CRADLE DUMP OCCASIONALLY WAS USED TO DUMP COAL.

UNDER NORMAL CIRCUMSTANCES, HOWEVER, LOADED COAL CARS PROCEEDED OVER THE CRADLE DUMP AND ONTO THE PHILLIPS CAR RETARDER (7) AND CROSSOVER DUMP (8) (PHILLIPS CAR CO, PITTSBURGH, PA). THE CAR RETARDER RELEASED CARS INDIVIDUALLY ONTO THE CROSSOVER DUMP, WHERE THEY WERE TIPPED FORWARD AND EMPTIED INTO A HOPPER (9). A RECIPROCATING FEEDER (10) AT THE BOTTOM OF THE HOPPER FED THE COAL INTO THE MAIN STORAGE BIN VIA ONE OF TWO ROUTES. IF THE BOTTOM OF THE FEEDER WAS OPEN, THE COAL PASSED STRAIGHT THROUGH ONTO THE BRINK OF THE MAIN STORAGE BIN (11). IF THE BOTTOM OF THE FEEDER WAS CLOSED, THE COAL WAS DISTRIBUTED ONTO AN APRON CONVEYOR (12) THAT LOWERED THE COAL MORE GENTLY INTO THE BOTTOM OF THE BIN. ONCE EMPTIED, THE COAL CARS MOVED FORWARD TO THE SWITCHBACK (13) AT THE FRONT OF THE HEADHOUSE AND TRANS- FERRED ONTO THE "CREEPER TRACK", WHERE THE CREEPER SNAGGED THE BOTTOM OF THE EMPTY CAR AND CARRIED IT BACK INTO THE MINE TO BE PICKED UP BY THE HAULAGE LOCOMOTIVE. IF A CAR WAS IN NEED OF REPAIR, IT WAS SWITCHED ONTO A TRACK THAT BYPASSED THE CREEPER TRACK AND LED INTO THE CAR REPAIR SHOP.

IN THE MEANTIME, COAL IN THE MAIN STORAGE BIN WAS BEING FED THROUGH CHUTES INTO THE MONITOR CARS FOR THE TRIP DOWN SLOPE TO THE PROCESSING PLANT AT THE TRACK LEVEL.

For information on purchasing reproductions of any of the photos or drawings in this book contact the Chesapeake & Ohio Historical Society Archives
312 East Ridgeway Street - Clifton Forge, VA - 24422 - 540-862-2210 or email cohs@cohs.org

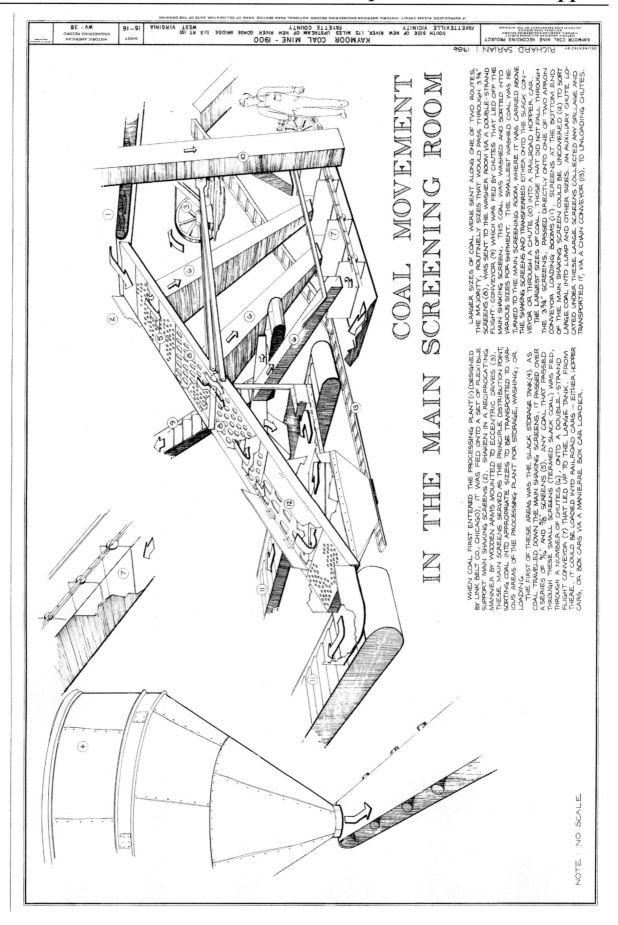

COAL MOVEMENT
IN THE MAIN SCREENING ROOM

WHEN COAL FIRST ENTERED THE PROCESSING PLANT(1)(DESIGNED BY LINK BELT CO., CHICAGO), IT WAS FED ONTO A SET OF FLEXIBLE SUPPORT MAIN SHAKING SCREENS (2). SHAKEN IN A RECIPROCATING MANNER BY WOODEN ARMS MOUNTED TO ECCENTRIC DRIVES (3), THESE MAIN SCREENS SERVED AS THE PRINCIPLE DISTRIBUTION POINT, SORTING COAL INTO APPROPRIATE SIZES TO BE TRANSPORTED TO VARIOUS AREAS OF THE PROCESSING PLANT FOR STORAGE, WASHING, OR LOADING.

THE FIRST OF THESE AREAS WAS THE SLACK STORAGE TANK(4). AS COAL TRAVELED DOWN THE MAIN SHAKING SCREENS, IT PASSED OVER A SERIES OF ¾" AND ⅝" SCREENS (5). ANY COAL THAT PASSED THROUGH THESE SMALL SCREENS (TERMED SLACK COAL) WAS FED, THROUGH A NUMBER OF CHUTES (6), ONTO A DOUBLE-STRAND FLIGHT CONVEYOR (7) THAT LED UP TO THE LARGE TANK. FROM THERE, IT COULD BE LOADED INTO RAILROAD CARS — EITHER HOPPER CARS, OR BOX CARS VIA A MANIERE BOX CAR LOADER.

LARGER SIZES OF COAL WERE SENT ALONG ONE OF TWO ROUTES. THE MAJORITY, ROUTINELY SIZES THAT WOULD PASS THROUGH 3¾" SCREENS (8), WAS SENT TO THE WASHER ROOM VIA A DOUBLE-STRAND FLIGHT-CONVEYOR (9) WHICH WAS FED BY CHUTES THAT LED OFF THE MAIN SHAKING SCREEN. THIS COAL WAS WASHED AND SORTED INTO VARIOUS SIZES FOR SHIPMENT. THE SMALLEST WASHED COAL WAS RETURNED TO THE MAIN SCREENING ROOM, WHERE IT WAS CARRIED ABOVE THE SHAKING SCREENS AND TRANSFERRED EITHER ONTO THE SLACK CONVEYOR, OR THROUGH A CHUTE (10) INTO A RAILROAD HOPPER CAR.

THE LARGEST SIZES OF COAL, THOSE THAT DID NOT FALL THROUGH THE 3¾" SCREENS, PASSED DIRECTLY ONTO ONE OF TWO APRON CONVEYOR LOADING BOOMS (11). SCREENS AT THE BOTTOM END OF THE MAIN SHAKING SCREEN COULD BE UNCOVERED (12) TO SORT LARGE COAL INTO LUMP AND OTHER SIZES. AN AUXILIARY CHUTE, LOCATED UNDER THESE LARGE SCREENS COLLECTED ANY SPILLAGE AND TRANSPORTED IT, VIA A CHAIN CONVEYOR (13), TO UNLOADING CHUTES.

NOTE : NO SCALE

DELINEATED BY
RICHARD SARIAN : 1986

UNITED STATES DEPARTMENT OF THE INTERIOR
NATIONAL PARK SERVICE
HISTORIC AMERICAN ENGINEERING RECORD
KAYMOOR COAL MINE RECORDING PROJECT

KAYMOOR COAL MINE - 1900
SOUTH SIDE OF NEW RIVER, 1.75 MILES UPSTREAM OF NEW RIVER GORGE BRIDGE (US RT 19)
FAYETTEVILLE VICINITY   FAYETTE COUNTY   WEST VIRGINIA

HISTORIC AMERICAN ENGINEERING RECORD   SHEET   15 OF 16   WV - 38

IF REPRODUCED, PLEASE CREDIT HISTORIC AMERICAN ENGINEERING RECORD, NATIONAL PARK SERVICE, NAME OF DELINEATOR, DATE OF THE DRAWING

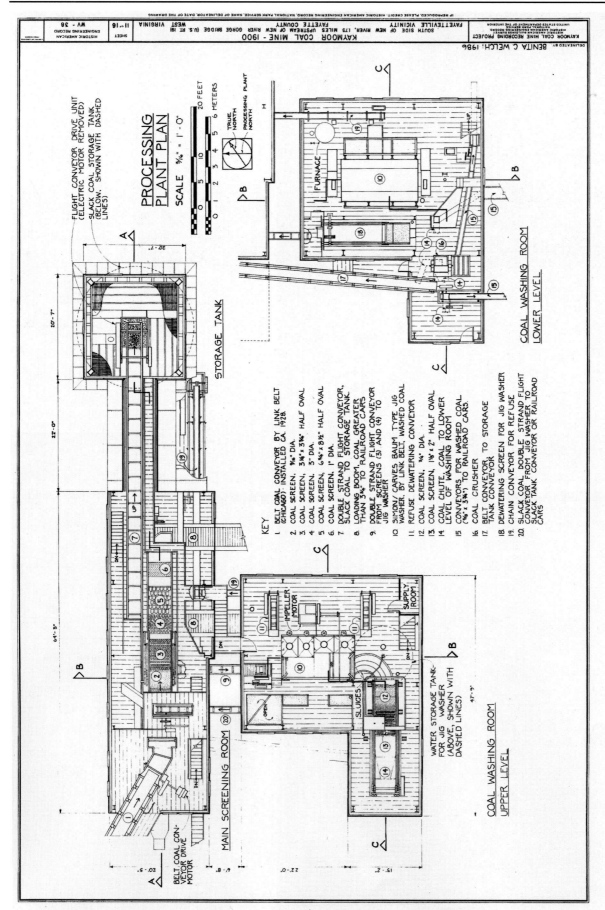

PROCESSING PLANT PLAN

SCALE ³⁄₁₆" = 1'-0"

STORAGE TANK

MAIN SCREENING ROOM

COAL WASHING ROOM
UPPER LEVEL

COAL WASHING ROOM
LOWER LEVEL

PROCESSING PLANT NORTH

TRUE NORTH

FLIGHT CONVEYOR DRIVE UNIT (ELECTRIC MOTOR REMOVED)
SLACK COAL STORAGE TANK (BELOW, SHOWN WITH DASHED LINES)

BELT COAL CONVEYOR DRIVE MOTOR

WATER STORAGE TANK FOR JIG WASHER (ABOVE, SHOWN WITH DASHED LINES)

FURNACE

SUPPLY ROOM

IMPELLER MOTOR

SLUICES

OPEN

KEY

1. BELT COAL CONVEYOR BY LINK BELT (CHICAGO), INSTALLED CA. 1928.
2. COAL SCREEN, ⁵⁄₁₆" DIA.
3. COAL SCREEN, 3¼" x 3¾" HALF OVAL
4. COAL SCREEN, 5" DIA.
5. COAL SCREEN, 6¼" x 8½" HALF OVAL
6. COAL SCREEN, 1" DIA.
7. DOUBLE STRAND FLIGHT CONVEYOR, SLACK COAL TO STORAGE TANK
8. LOADING BOOM, COAL GREATER THAN 3¼" TO RAILROAD CARS
9. DOUBLE STRAND FLIGHT CONVEYOR FROM SCREENS (3) AND (4) TO JIG WASHER
10. SIMON/ CARVES BAUM TYPE JIG WASHER, BY LINK BELT, WASHED COAL
11. REFUSE DEWATERING CONVEYOR
12. COAL SCREEN, ³⁄₄" DIA.
13. COAL SCREEN, 1⅝" x 2" HALF OVAL
14. COAL CHUTE, COAL TO LOWER LEVEL OF WASHING ROOM
15. CONVEYORS FOR WASHED COAL (⁵⁄₁₆" x 3¾") TO RAILROAD CARS.
16. COAL CRUSHER
17. BELT CONVEYOR, TO STORAGE TANK CONVEYOR
18. DEWATERING SCREEN FOR JIG WASHER
19. CHAIN CONVEYOR FOR REFUSE
20. SLACK COAL DOUBLE STRAND FLIGHT CONVEYOR FROM JIG WASHER TO SLACK TANK CONVEYOR OR RAILROAD CARS

HISTORIC AMERICAN ENGINEERING RECORD | SHEET 11 OF 16 | WV - 38

SOUTH SIDE OF NEW RIVER, 175 MILES UPSTREAM OF NEW RIVER GORGE BRIDGE (U.S. RT. 19)

KAYMOOR COAL MINE - 1900

FAYETTEVILLE VICINITY   FAYETTE COUNTY   WEST VIRGINIA

UNITED STATES DEPARTMENT OF THE INTERIOR
HISTORIC AMERICAN ENGINEERING RECORD
NATIONAL PARK SERVICE
KAYMOOR COAL MINE RECORDING PROJECT

DELINEATED BY BENITA C. WELCH, 1986

For information on purchasing reproductions of any of the photos or drawings in this book contact the Chesapeake & Ohio Historical Society Archives
312 East Ridgeway Street - Clifton Forge, VA - 24422 - 540-862-2210 or email cohs@cohs.org

HINTON AND HUNTINGTON DIVISIONS

Central Region
ASHLAND-RUSSELL DIVISION
HOCKING DIVISION
TOLEDO TERMINAL DIVISION

These maps taken from C&O employee timetables show the railway's coal lines and can be used to identify the branches and subdivisions mentioned in the photo captions in this chapter. The Hinton and Huntington Division map covers the coal branches between Hinton and Barboursville, which include the major lines in the Greenbrier, New River, Raleigh, Coal River, and Logan fields. The Ashland Division map shows the Big Sandy District in Kentucky. North of it (west by railroad direction) are seen the Hocking coalfields lines southeast of Columbus. This book contains no treatment of this region since it was largely exhausted by the 1930s.

FOR BETTER SERVICE

C&O's new $7 million Toledo coal loader... fastest in the world... cuts turnaround time for lake freighters.

AND BETTER COAL

The finest bituminous coal for every purpose comes from the territory served by C&O...The Coal Bin of America

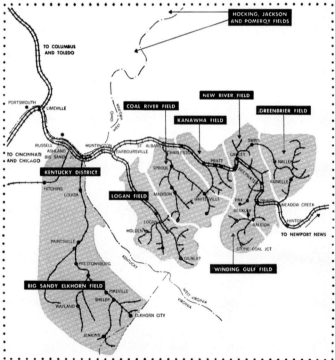

For dependable deliveries of top quality coals, contact coal producers on the C&O. And for specific help in meeting your own fuel requirements, write to: R. C. Riedinger, General Coal Traffic Manager, Chesapeake and Ohio Railway Co., Terminal Tower, Cleveland 1, Ohio.

Chesapeake and Ohio Railway

WORLD'S LARGEST CARRIER OF BITUMINOUS COAL

This 1959 advertisement touts C&O's new Toledo coal loader and uses the "Coal Bin of America" slogan that was begun right after World War II. (C&OHS Collection)

A house for tomorrow

When Bill Miller first talked to the architect about his new home he stressed his desire to put into it the soundest materials and the newest conveniences.

"I hope my grandchildren will be happy in this house," he explained. "New improvements come fast these days, so let's try to be a few years ahead in our planning."

"What fuel would you like to use?" asked the architect when the discussion reached the heating plant.

"I would prefer to use coal," answered Bill, "I understand it is the most economical fuel here, as it is in most areas. But I don't want my wife

to be a furnace-tender."

"With a modern, bin-feed stoker with thermostatic control," said the architect, "your heating will be completely automatic, as well as clean and convenient. And coal has some big advantages — it gives a steady heat, not an off-again-on-again heat. Then there's this for the fellow who looks ahead: I don't know how long these other fuels are going to last. Every year they have to drill their wells deeper, and we are becoming more and more dependent on foreign supplies. As these other fuels get scarcer, they are going to get even more expensive.

"But coal is another story. There is plenty of coal right here in the United States to last us for hundreds—maybe thousands of years. That's something to think about when you're planning a house with the hope that your grandchildren will still be living in it."

Bring your fuel problems to C&O

As the world's largest carrier of bituminous coal, the C&O is intimately familiar with every phase of coal use. We have a large staff of experts who will gladly help you to locate the coal best suited to your needs; to help you use it most efficiently; to help get it to you promptly.

Write to:
Coal Traffic Department
Chesapeake and Ohio Railway
2105 Terminal Tower
Cleveland 1, Ohio

Chesapeake and Ohio Railway

COAL — FUEL OF THE FUTURE

WHY CHES

SUPERIOR COAL. The naturally high q specifications by modern methods and equip vertical screens which do the job with a mini

SUPERIOR SERVICE. Chesapeake and keeps 99% of them operating by its prompt r ample power keep the cars rolling to insure o

For dependable deliveries of top quality coals, contact on the C&O. And for specific help in meeting your own fu write to: R. C. Riedinger, General Coal Traffic Manage and Ohio Railway Co., Terminal Tower, Cleveland 1, Ohi

Chesapeake and Railway

WORLD'S LARGEST CARRIER OF BITUMIN

C&O constantly advertised its major product: coal. Innovative material such that as contained in these ads was a hallmark of the company's enthusiastic, creative, and highly focused advertising department. C&O's public relations and advertising program was at the forefront of this type of activity not only within railroading, but within American industrial advertising overall. (C&OHS Collection).